A WILD TASTE

HARRY BEWICK

A WILD TASTE

A Methuen Paperback

First published in Great Britain 1958
by Peter Davies Ltd
This paperback edition published 1987
by Methuen London Ltd
11 New Fetter Lane, London EC4P 4EE
© 1958 Harry Bewick

Printed in Great Britain
by Richard Clay Ltd, Bungay, Suffolk

British Library Cataloguing in Publication Data

Bewick, Harry
    A wild taste.
    1. Country life—Ireland   2. Ireland—
    Social life and customs—20th century
    I. Title
    941.7′009′734   DA959.1

    ISBN 0-413-15730-X

CONTENTS

1 ENGLAND

I WAS on the way to Hertfordshire with my two daughters Stella and Joey. I was taking Stella to a progressive school in Letchworth and intended to buy a house there so that she would be a day-girl instead of a boarder.

The train journey was long and tedious—I was obliged to talk because Stella aged nine, with her flaming red curls, hyper-sensitive face and long boyish figure attracted the attention of the other passengers. Joey was four—although she had none of the beauty and jumpy nerves of her sister she also attracted attention with her straw-coloured hair, black eyes and bursting-with-health appearance.

So it was a relief to step out on to the platform at the end of the journey, put our luggage into the station office, and walk out into the street and be in the fresh air. The only thing I knew about Letchworth was its position on the map, which showed it to be in the centre of Hertforshire, but this knowledge didn't prevent me from feeling that we were at a sea-side place, and that if we walked down the street we would come to the centre of things : the promenade, the sea and the crowds. And I really wasn't far wrong, because on turning a corner at the bottom, we came upon a large paddling pool serpentining through flat stones and fine grass and full of shouting children. Stella and Joey kicked off their sandals and ran into it before I had time to speak, so I sat down under a tree laden with

7

may and looked around. I didn't allow myself to
think for one moment that a garden city wasn't really
what I wanted for myself or for the children; instead
I thought it a nice place, and I sat smelling the may
and lilac from the surrounding trees and watching the
millions of sparrows swirling about like leaves in a high
wind and settling, tweeting noisily, to pick up the
crumbs the children had strewn on the grass; and I
listened to the trains in the distance shunting and toot-
ing like toy-town.

I held my face up to the hot sun, and I was very
soon lulled into unconsciousness.

I awakened with a cold shudder to see the sun
sinking behind the houses opposite. My first thoughts
were that we still had no place to stay, and then, were
the children all right? I was relieved to see them playing in the pool, so I called to them to stay where they
were until I came back, and I hurried off and rang the
bell at the first place I saw, "The Garden City Hotel,"
just across the road. A young black-haired woman
wearing horn-rimmed glasses came to the door. "I'm
very sorry Madam," she said, "we only came into this
hotel ourselves last week and we have the painters in
at present—we won't be opening for another month.
I'm very sorry, Madam. . . ." I began to feel a little
panicky at being turned away and I saw myself knocking at door after door without any result and the
children crying with tiredness. Someone was shouting,
"Madam, madam," but it hardly registered until it
was repeated several more times. Then I turned round
and saw the woman from the hotel running after me,
"Madam." I was never in my life called "Madam" so
much and I felt it didn't suit me.

"If you wouldn't mind the state of the place perhaps

I could find a room for you somewhere. It's unlucky to turn away the first guest, you know, Madam."

I didn't know, but I was both surprised and relieved. By the time I had collected the luggage from the station and brought the children from the paddling pool it was growing dark and inside the hotel it was still darker. We tripped over rolled-up carpets and paint cans, and peered into dim rooms with dust sheets covering mounds of furniture, as the young proprietress talked away like a babbling brook in an accent I thought was American, but not quite—it was much prettier and very fast. She showed us into a room at the end of a long passage, and told me to come to the kitchen as soon as I had put the children to bed, apologising because all the other rooms were in a turmoil.

I found her sitting on top of the Aga cooker drinking tea, away down in the belly of the hotel. She offered me a cup and a seat beside her on the warm oven top. Under these conditions it was difficult to keep up all the "Madams" and she soon dropped them and asked my name. "You're not to keep that name," she said horrified, "you must change it. That's my name too, and I never had any luck until I changed it to 'Patsy'. I know! I'll call you 'Harry'," she said laughing. "When we want someone to blame we always say 'Harry did it.'" She told me she was Irish and came from County Kerry. When once these preliminaries were over she began to speak of what lay next to her heart and I listened to her beautiful lilting accent and husky voice telling me about Ireland for hour after hour.

Eventually I did buy a house, and the evening before we were to move in Patsy brought up a new subject. Something that was to alter the whole of our lives.

She told me about her niece and nephew who lived on the side of a mountain in Kerry with their Uncle "Sticks", a postman.

"They were all right while their Grandmother was alive," Patsy said softly, "but she died a year ago and the children are on their own most of the time because Sticks is out all day on the post, and every evening he is in the pubs drinking. They are only eight and nine years old and I worry about them a lot—God help them, the poor children!"

Their father was Patsy's brother, and he had got TB with being on the run in the mountains during the Troubles. Their mother had developed it after, and they both died within a few weeks of each other.

"I'll go and look after them," I said impulsively.

"Don't be so silly, Harry. How can you when you've just bought a house and Stella has just begun her new school?"

"You can let the house for me and surely there's a school in Kerry she can go to." I felt possessed, and Patsy, too, acted as though the fates were leading her, gently, but quite firmly.

Without hesitation she wrote off immediately to the tenant on her farm in Kenmare, in Kerry, to tell her that the place would be needed for an English woman and her two children, and before the ink on the envelope was dry it was lying at the bottom of the letter box waiting to cross the Irish Sea.

2 THE JOURNEY

It was October before everything was arranged for us to go to Ireland.

Patsy came with us to see us settle in. We left from Euston and although I knew the journey would be long and uninteresting, we were all excited, except Patsy, who had done it so many times before. The children behaved themselves all the way, but when we arrived at Holyhead at two o'clock in the morning and saw the big hulk of the mail-boat standing in the oily water, and smelt the strong salty wind, there was no holding them back. As soon as we crossed the gang-plank, they were off to explore the boat. After Patsy and I had dealt with the luggage we stood by the deck rails waiting for the boat to leave. Soon the engines began to throb and the water to churn, while men rushed about shouting instructions and casting off ropes. We stood for a while and watched the dimly-lit docks slipping by, then we went into the saloon out of the cold wind. The heat, and the smell of beer and ham-sandwiches, met us as we stepped inside. A drunk was playing the melodeon and singing "Galway Bay". A group of nuns and priests were talking and laughing hilariously, which surprised me. There were also lots of worried-looking mothers with children of all ages. Stella and Joey ran back and forth to tell us what they had seen; "people asleep on shelves with curtains in front of them, and 'postmen' walking about every-where." Someone asked them if they were going to

Ballybunion, and this name amused them for the rest
of the journey.

Sleep was out of the question. The only time the
children sat down was when we had tea and toast,
in the dining-room—to them it tasted quite unlike any
other tea and toast, even to me it did—We arrived
at Dun Laoghaire at six o'clock in the morning, with
a bitterly cold wind whipping up the sea; we had to
shield our tired eyes against the glare of the sun
splintering and sparkling on the ripples.

Some of our luggage was missing and we spent so
much time trying to find it that we missed our connec-
tion south and had to drag our bags to some obscure
platform. The train there looked about a mile long and
only about half-a-dozen people got into it. The children stood up on the iron-hard upholstery and looked
over the top of the rough partitions to the whole length
of the carriage—they were thrilled, but Patsy wasn't.
She was furious to think we could have been speeding
south on a smart Pullman and enjoying a delicious
lunch *en route*—it was more than she could bear to
think about, so I hardly dared open my mouth. We
were in Ireland—and that was all that mattered to me.

We had to pull up three times at every station
because the train was too long for the short platforms.
Even when no one got out, the ritual of porters waving
flags, running up the platforms, shouting and blowing
whistles was still performed. At each station, milk-cans
were hurled in or hurled out. The thud of them hitting
the floor of the van shuddered through the whole
length of the train and vibrated into our brains. The
milk-cans seemed to be all that mattered and the passengers were ignored. I felt it was only by a favour
that we were allowed there and we hadn't to make any

demands. We drank sweet watery tea and ate limp
Marie biscuits at every station which boasted a tea-
room—always keeping an eye on our part of the train
in case it should rattle off without us.

After sitting in that compartment for fourteen hours
we became one with the train, rocking, lurching and
allowing every jangle to pass through us without resis-
tance. It seemed our whole life without any hope of
deliverance. Then in no-man's-land, a porter breezed
in and through our stupor we heard him telling us
that the train went no further.

"In heaven's name, where are we?" Patsy said to
him.

" 'Tis in Mallow ye are, Ma'am."

"And what's the time?"

" 'Tis half after tin."

"And what time is the next train to Kenmare?"

"Shure, there's not a one at this time o'night;
Monday noon will be the nixt."

And this was Saturday! I saw Patsy disappearing
into a telephone box and, after quite a long time, she
came out in a raging temper.

"The so-and-so's! . . . If this was in England
they'd have to pull themselves together! I've been trying to get someone to come for us in a car and devil a
one will turn out. We just can't stay in Mallow—it's a
dreadful place—only one long street and it without
a decent hotel in the whole run of it."

Just then another train pulled up on the same
platform where our train had been.

"Where's this train going?" Patsy shouted to a
porter.

"Killarney," he shouted as he ran past us.

"Come on, Harry! We'll go to Killarney."

We hurriedly boarded the train and after a short journey we arrived at eleven o'clock and went straight to the International Hotel and up the stairs to bed. Such comfort was unbelievable! I never knew before that beds could be so soft, so clean, so light with eiderdown and so warm with a hot bottle; but sleep had to be postponed for some time until the cinema across the road closed down. The night air was jumping with the shouts of frenzied gangsters.

The next morning we wakened to blue skies and sweet tempers. After breakfast Patsy said that we might as well see something of Killarney now that we were stuck there till Monday. So we set off to walk to Ross Castle; through the town, which I could hardly believe was "Heaven's Reflex"; being Sunday, I suppose it looked its worst with all the shops closed and very few people about. Then we turned off the main road on to a path that led through a wood. Immediately everything changed! We were walking in a new world—uncontaminated. Something was in the air—something indescribable! Patsy changed too; all her acquired English ways left her and she became Irish right through, singing Irish songs that blended with the scenery and relating the legend of 'Tir-na-nOg', the Land of Perpetual Youth which lay under the lake water. If you were out in the bright moon you'd see a group of white horses standing under the young oaks on the hill. They'd gallop up to you and if you wished, you could be taken on their backs right down under to Tir-na-nOg and partake for ever of eternal youth. On this, our first day, we were being shown the very heart of Ireland. How lucky we were to have come with Patsy!

When we reached Ross Castle we climbed the winding stone stairs and stood out on the battlements and looked across the lake, which was studded with small rocky islands, to the misty blue mountains beyond. The beauty there was unearthly but at the same time strangely tangible. On the walk back—along the road this time—we got talking to some of the local boys who told us that there was a hurling match that day between Kenmare and Killarney and that a special train was being run to take the players and their supporters back home. Patsy immediately decided that we would go on that train too, and we did, packed in amongst a crowd of victorious drunks. At Kenmare everyone sprayed out on the platform, including us, feeling as drunk as the rest.

We went straight to the Muxna Hotel because Patsy had been to school with the proprietor and if we had gone anywhere else, he would have been offended. "The Muxnas", as everyone called them, had so many children running around the hotel I couldn't count them and most of them had whooping-cough. No one seemed to care, least of all the children themselves who were dashing along the passages playing a game called "Hunting" and coughing until they were sick. Stella and Joey were pulled into the game and in no time they too were shouting "Cot" like the others whenever they "caught" somebody.

We were the only people in the hotel but we were given only one room. Patsy had a bed to herself but I had to share the other one with the children. It troughed in the middle and was hell! but as Patsy and I never got to bed before dawn for the two weeks we were there, it was hardly worth complaining. We spent every evening in the kitchen reminiscing with Patsy's old friends and hiding whatever drinks we were having whenever a knock came on the door. Everyone started making for home at five in the morning but not because they were tired—there was no flagging in the conversation or the laughter until the last one had left.

3 KENMARE

I was awakened by a loud clap of thunder and I thought the roof of the hotel had been hit. I got up and, wrapping the eiderdown round me, I went to look out of the open window. Although it was early morning, it looked like the middle of the night; I could just distinguish a mass of moving cattle, and men with sacks over their heads, on the street below. The smell of wet sacking, hay and cows floated up into the bedroom. Thunder was rumbling and dying out in the distance and dogs were howling. I heard a whack on an animal's hide and an angry voice blaspheming, "Git up outa that! God blasht ye for a cow." Then the animals stopped making a noise, the men stopped cursing and the thunder ceased. There was a heavy silence as though the world were breathing in. I sat, not daring to stir. Then, like a revelation, a demon escaped from the centre of the earth and tore the black cloth of the sky with barbed talons charged with electricity. Forked lightning, electric blue, streaked from top to bottom down the sky, and before it had earthed almost, came the thunder, crackling and exploding. Everything was zizzing with electric current and I found myself lifting my hands off the sill. The same demon, still at large, with glee and viciousness, pulled back a trapdoor in the sky and down sluiced the rain in a solid mass. A voice inside me said, Tir-na-nOg, and I was under the lakes and was being given eternal youth.

17

My introduction to Kenmare was like shaking hands with the Gods.

Everyone was beginning to waken up and no one had heard the storm; I had been privileged to feel the heart-beat of Ireland; it was worth coming all those hundreds of miles, for this alone, I thought.

After breakfast, Patsy took us out into the town and, I think, introduced us to every single person. It was fair day, and everyone had come in from the surrounding country, including all Patsy's friends and relations. They were, all of them, very interested and curious to hear about us. They shook hands and said "Welcome to Ireland" and invited us to visit them. Everyone was called Sullivan, and then, as soon as their backs were turned, Patsy called them by some other name such as Juff-Jaff, Batty-Bat, Chapel-Din, Hanny-Dinny, Dinny-Island, Guiney-Gow, Jimmy-the-Master, Dan-Pa-Jack, Bina-the-Point, Dan-the-Head, Tim-Timothy, Willy-Bess, Michael-Post-Office—never-ending nicknames to distinguish one Sullivan from another. I was in a daze. Every shop was also a pub, where the men were drinking and the women doing their shopping. Kenmare itself was sunk in a hollow and looked wet and sad; the mountains all round were navy blue, and there was a wild yellow sky overhead. Although the rain had stopped, everything still looked stormy. It was a bad day for my first impressions, except of course of the people who were very alive and warm-hearted. I noticed that everyone was on equal terms; no one was better than anyone else, whatever their job—even the Boots in the Lansdown Hotel was on equal terms with the guests. He was kneeling and blowing up the turf fire when we went in for a cup of tea, and he turned to us and said:

" 'Tis quinched altogether, faith, 'tis as black as the hobs o' hell."

We went back to the Muxna Hotel for lunch. Patsy had explained beforehand that we were vegetarians— an unheard-of-thing—and that we would have pota- toes and whatever vegetable was going, raw and grated. At our place in the dining-room was laid a newspaper and on it the largest parsnip I had ever seen and next to it a tin grater. We were the biggest joke in years, "scratching at our vegetables," but we came off better than Patsy who had "crubeens" (pigs' feet) which she was swallowing in lumps for fear of offend- ing her old school pal by leaving any. After lunch, we went out into the street again. Most of the cattle had been sold and taken away. The street musicians and tricksters were coming out of the pubs after having spent all they had made, by the look of them. Old women in black shawls were untying their orange- painted donkey-cars from the railings of the square and going away, loaded with bulging sacks, farm implements, pots and pans, and so forth. The stalls which had been set up in the square, were being dis- mantled and loaded on to lorries. The tinkers had stopped trying to sell rosary beads and paper flowers. An old man was walking down the middle of the street ringing a bell and announcing that a bull had gone astray and that if anyone saw it, would they report it to the Guards. All the fun was over and every- one going home, so we went back to the hotel to see what was going on there. We were glad to get in off the streets as we could hardly keep our feet from slipping in the wet cow dung left behind from the fair.

4 VISITING

THE next day Patsy hired a car to take us to her cousins at Gleninchaquin.

We started off by going through the town and over the Bell Height—Patsy telling us the names of all the places as we passed by. After passing over a white, arched bridge which spanned an inlet of the sea, but which was called on the map 'Kenmare River', we turned sharp right, the road then ran through woods where gigantic foreign-looking trees grew near the road edge, then out into the open again with a vast view of the sea and the Macgillicuddy Reeks.

The road ran near to the sea for several miles. Then turning left we began to climb through a range of mountains, passing small white-washed farms crouched in rock-strewn land where Kerry cows and donkeys were nibbling at the sparse grass that grew between the heather and rocks. Turf was stacked up against the end walls as high as the houses themselves. There was an invigorating smell of wet bog-land and heather. Sea birds and curlews were soaring in the air that was full of space and loneliness. When we reached Gleninchaquin, the road ran so near to the lake in places that the water washed over the car wheels. Patsy pointed to a heap of rubble on the far side of the lake, "Look, Harry! That's where I was born; we were evicted from it when I was a child and no one has bothered about it since." It was a lonely place on the edge of the lake and at the foot of the mountains.

At the top of the lake the road came to an end so the driver drove the car on to the grass and we walked on a path that led through the heather to the farm.

Patsy's cousins were standing at their door waiting to welcome us—Irish girls one reads about, black curly hair, large grey eyes and complexions like wild roses. They had just finished churning, they said, giving each of us a mug to dip into the barrel churn for the buttermilk. It tasted like lemon juice mixed through thick cream.

Then we sat down to tea at the long kitchen table laid with a white starched damask cloth patterned with pale grey ivy leaves. The cups and saucers were of thin fluted china—white with gold rims. Pink glass jugs and sugar basins were filled with thick bubbly cream and coarse yellow-tinted sugar. Dinner plates were stacked high with different kinds of home-made breads; soda-bread, yellow-meal bread and barn-brack. There was a square of heather honey from their own hives and rounds of butter stamped with acorns and oak leaves. The two girls waited on us, pouring out strong piping-hot tea from an earthenware pot, and we were helped over our shoulders to boiled eggs spooned straight out of the pan. Everything was old-fashioned, wholesome and plentiful.

After tea I went to the door to look around. A mountain towered into the sky, dwarfing the farm. A cascade of water fell from its heights joining a river which ran into the lake. The wind caught at its surface and drove a sheet of thin mist across the face of the other mountains. It looked like a lace curtain billowing in the wind. Other mountains were covered in pine trees and ran steep and sheer into the lake and reflected into the water cut by blades of shining silver and gold. The scenery was majestic but not remote; it seemed at one with the homely farms and people.

The girls' father built up the fire with turf, stacking it round a burning tree trunk, the rest of it stuck out into the middle of the room, and he kept kicking it further in as it burnt away. We sat on two long timber seats, smooth and shining like silk with use, and listened to the father and Patsy reminiscing about the old days when she was a child and lived across the lake. The children fell asleep but still Patsy and the father went on talking hour after hour and I listened to them telling of their strange experiences with banshees, leprechauns and fairies. These appeared to be strange mystic beings linking the people both to the earth, the sky, and the elements, and to death and the unknown world.

It was after midnight when we carried the children to the car, and they went on sleeping as we drove back with the moon shining on the lake like a ball of yellow gold. They never knew that night how they got to bed.

The next day Patsy hired the car and driver again to take us to see her friends at Ardgroom, a small town near the open Atlantic. We took the same road as we did the day before but, instead of turning up into the mountains, we drove near to the sea all the way. We arrived to find the house locked up and the town deserted.

Eventually, we saw an old man who told us that everyone was at the funeral of an old woman who had died at the age of 102. He told us how to get to the chapel and we were soon in the crowd that filled the road. Some were on bikes and others on donkey-cars, horse-cars and on foot. Everyone was laughing and talking gaily. Death seemed as natural to them as the heather fading on the side of the mountains. As soon as we entered the chapel, however, everyone at once became serious and full of respect. I felt I ought not to be there as I couldn't follow any of the complicated ritual. I saw for.the first time, men on their knees praying and somehow, although it appeared feminine to me, it also made them look more manly.

After it was over we found Patsy's friends in the crowd outside the chapel; they thought we weren't coming as we were an hour late according to their time. We should have enquired when we made the appointment if they followed summer time or not, as everyone in Kerry pleased themselves about changing the clocks.

After a meal we set off, each with a sack, to gather carrageen moss from the rocks. As we passed a cottage half hidden in the rocky foreland, two young girls came leaping down on to the road and asked us where we were going because they wanted to come along too. One of them lifted Joey up on her back and jumped from rock to rock, as sure-footed as a mountain-goat. The wind raged at their torn clothes and long, uncombed hair, making them look as wild and fey as the scenery around them. They shouted in Gaelic to a young man who was fishing with a rod made from a silver birch tree-trunk. His line billowed twenty feet down to the green sea below and to where the waves splashed up against the rocks and veered back, making maps of swirling white foam. We sat behind a rock, sheltered from the wind, waiting for the tide to turn. Down below us was a cement platform, built on the strand, and the girls told us that they used to dance there every night to the melodeon before they built the new dance hall in Ardgroom.

At last the tide had receded enough for us to paddle into the shallow water and pull the wet carrageen from the rocks. When we got it home it had to be spread out to dry and bleach in the sun, then packed away for use in the winter; it was supposed to keep away colds when boiled in milk and taken hot. As we left Ardgroom we could hear the ceilidhe music coming from the new dance hall and, above it all, the thump of feet and the laughter of the dancers.

We were all very excited when at last it was time to visit Mary and Timmy—Patsy's niece and nephew. By now, everyone in Kenmare knew that Patsy had brought over 'a foreign woman' to look after them, but whether or not Sticks, or the children themselves, knew about it, was another matter. When we got to Lauraugh, which was twelve miles outside Kenmare, we sent the driver into the National School to ask them to come out and see their Auntie Patsy. We sat in the car, waiting, and very soon two children came running down the slope, followed by the smiling driver. Patsy talked and joked with them in her usual cheery way but it was all beyond them. Their big grey eyes peeped up at her and deep furrows scored their brows. They were barefoot and thinly dressed and looked perished with the cold.

"I've a good mind to pack them into the car this very minute and take them back to the hotel for hot baths and get them into warm jerseys," Patsy said, but no sooner were these words out of her mouth than Sticks—their uncle—seemed to rise up out of the ground and was standing there with his large hands on the children's shoulders. He looked quite sinister in his long black postman's greatcoat piped with green and fastened up to the neck with silver-harp buttons. He was warm and dry, anyway, with the exception of his black curly hair which was beaded with rain. He had a gaunt face and when he spoke he showed big square yellow teeth. He looked with hatred at Patsy. Angry words, wind and rain were all raging at once. The children were frightened; they couldn't understand what was going on between their Uncle and their Auntie Patsy. He made it quite clear, there and then, that he'd never let the children go.

On the way back we were so depressed we hardly spoke.

"Well, Harry, you've come all this way on a wild-goose chase. I suppose we'll all have to go back to England again."

But I knew that I wasn't going back to England again, even if Mary and Timmy never came to live with us.

5 THE FARM

WE had put off going to see Patsy's farm because it
was undergoing repairs but as she was due back in
England the following day, we decided to walk out
and have a look at it. We set out at eleven o'clock in
fine weather and had the whole day in front of us. We
went over the sea-bridge but, instead of taking The
Line—the main road by the sea—we climbed up on
to the Old Road. As this was only used by the few
people whose farms adjoined it, it was neglected.
Gorse bushes resembling young cactus plants were
beginning to take root between the stones; fungus that
looked like yellow stones pushed up through the pebbles, and rabbit-nibbled grass bordered the sides.
Swift flowing rivulets ran off the mountains over the
road then down the steep fields to the sea. As we passed
a low white-washed house, for which the road acted
as a farm-yard, a woman dressed in a long black skirt
and wearing men's boots, came out, and, putting her
hands up to her mouth, called "Eileen" in a long,
drawn-out wail. A huge bay horse was clanking and
hobbling awkwardly along the road with two of its
legs fettered with chains; donkeys were meandering
about or stretched out asleep in the middle of the road.
The view from this high road was too vast to take in
all at once. The sea lay below like spilt blue paint and
the mountains stood towering in the distant background. Their name—The Reeks—had a remote
sound and it was impossible to imagine any humans

climbing up to their summits. After crossing a peat-stained stream, Patsy gripped hold of my arm and pointed to a farm-house standing in the field below us.

"Look, Harry, there's your house! What do you think of it, eh?" My heart leapt into my ribs and although it was square and ugly, I loved it immediately. We went through a swing gate and down a field; then, after crossing a foot-bridge over the stream, we walked on past the cow-houses. Just as we reached the back-door, a young man came out pushing a wheel-barrow.

"How's the work getting along?" Patsy asked him.

"This avinin' will see me out of it. I just have to fix the floor in the room, then 'twill be finished, Ma'am."

We went into the kitchen which appeared to be the hub of the house; everything revolved round it. The back, front and "room" doors all led out of it, also the stairs which led up to two bedrooms with lime and timber walls. They had big windows back and front which came from the raftered ceiling right down to the floor boards, which meant we could lie in bed and see the view across the sea to the Reeks without any obstruction. The kitchen had a grey cement floor and the room was having a red cement floor put in by Paddy. In each room the walls were lime-washed. A few pieces of furniture were left behind by Bridie—the previous tenant—an old-fashioned timber bed, six deal chairs, an enormous oak flour chest, a dresser and a long seat like the one in Patsy's cousins' house; it also was worn to a silken smoothness. Patsy's sister had a farm a mile further along the road and, if we wanted any furniture out of it, we could take it as the house was unoccupied.

Patsy noticed some brown patches showing through

the lime-wash in the kitchen and as it had just been done, she asked Paddy for an explanation.

"Thim stains will come through no matter what ye do. Haven't I thim done thrice already."

"The woman can't live in the place if it's like this; it's like a slum," Patsy said to him crossly.

"Deed 'tis Ma'am, but what harrum, shure!" he said, walking out with a proud expression and his head held high.

"The cheeky fellow!" Patsy said, losing her temper —this wasn't the way workmen treated her in England. "Harry, you go out after him and tell him how you want it done. After all it's you who's going to live here."

I went out to where he was tearing down a perfectly good wall to lay under the cement in the room. I stood there, not knowing how to begin. If I'd cared all that much I suppose the words would have come but I was feeling so elated with everything I saw that I couldn't bring myself to telling anyone off. He looked up from his work and smiled from ear to ear. That finished it. I smiled back and walked back into the house and nothing was said.

The following day Patsy left for England and, after seeing her off, I hired a car to remove us out to the farm. We arrived to find Paddy clearing up his things ready to go but as soon as he saw us he put them down again and knelt on the floor and blew the fire up into a red glow and said he would make us a cup of tea. After filling the kettle up with stream water and hanging it on the hook at the back of the fire, he went out into the cow-house to where Bridie's cow was standing and milked it into a stout bottle. On the way past the hen-house, he went in and filled his pockets with

eggs and then started to make us a meal. He told us
that he had worked in England but he didn't like it
there. He played with the children and taught them
some steps of the Irish reel, playing the mouth-organ
at the same time. He was so witty he made us laugh
all the time. Then he left, saying that he would come
up the next day. The work was finished and I couldn't
think why he was coming but I said "All right."

The children were very excited, running in and out
of the house and splashing about in the stream while
I swilled the kitchen floor and made up the beds, pulling them right in front of the low windows.

Then just as it was getting dark, I noticed a man
chopping wood up by the cow-house. I was puzzled
and wondered if he knew that we had come to live
there. Perhaps, I thought, he was some relation of
Bridie's and lived in the house too. He piled the logs
on to his arms and walked towards the house and,
kicking the back door further open, he walked in and
went through to the room and let the logs drop on the
floor. I was waiting to say hello or something but
he was so pre-occupied that I hadn't a chance, so we
all stood in "the room" doorway and watched him as
he made up a fire. As soon as it was blazing, he picked
a log out of the flames, lit himself a cigarette, pulled
up a chair and sat down. Then he looked up at us for
the first time and said, "Hello, Ma'am." With this
slight encouragement I pulled up a chair too and sat
down. Were we visiting him or was he visiting us?
I just had to wait and see. He started a conversation
and I couldn't make out a single word of it. I made
several feeble replies and tried to vary them to pretend
I knew what he was saying. Then when he paused *I*
began to talk and *he* was nodding his head as though

he understood me. For over an hour we kept this up and I was still none the wiser as to who he was, what he was saying, or if he intended to leave or expected me to. Then, thank God, he got up and said, "Goodbye now, Ma'am." I understood this and "Hello, Ma'am" at the beginning but nothing else.

Later I found out that he was Mick Sullivan from the next farm. He told me that his mother had sent him down to "kindle a fire for the foreign woman who was without a sod of turf or a bit."

6 FIRST DAY ON THE FARM

THE children wakened the next morning still just as excited. They ran in and out of the house and explored the fields and stream. I was getting a meal ready when they came rushing in looking very scared. "There's a witch outside!" Stella said, pointing out of the back door.

An old woman, very thin, with an aquiline face, was striding down the fields towards the house. She was all in black and over her bent shoulders was a sack and she was carrying a big rough stick.

"Hello, Ma'am," she shouted when she saw me. "I have a few hins fer ye in the bag. I'll put thim here in the cabin until they gits to know the place." I watched her empty out a lot of feathers and hens on to the hen-house floor.

"Bridie has the hasps destroyed on ye," she said as she was latching the door behind her. " 'Tis better ye have yer own iggs than be robbed in thim bloody shops, yerra! They'll soon get used te the place, but kape thim in a while and I hope, Ma'am, they lays will fer ye."

"But I don't know anything about hens," I said, alarmed.

"What harrum! Ye'll soon learn, shure."

"I don't know what to give them to eat or anything," I went on.

"Give thim a handful of the coarse male mixed through the spuds. 'Twill do thim will, faith."

"But, how much?" I said, only understanding 'spuds'.

"What they don't ate, won't they lave behind, arra! Good-bye and good luck," she shouted.

I watched her going up to the old road, wondering who she was. It was very kind of her to bring me a present and I had never even thanked her, I realized —I'd been too scared at the thought of having hens to look after.

I was peeping at them through a crack in the door when I was startled by a man's voice shouting, "Hello, Ma'am, what arou doin' at all?"

It was Paddy, the man who had repaired the floor. I told him about the woman who had just gone and he said it would be Mrs Sullivan from the farm above.

"Ye have an ould stump of a tree in the haggard there," he said, "and I thought I'd come up and cut it down fer ye, and I'll bring ye a rail of turf from my bog thin, tegither with the wood ye'll be all right fer firin' this winter inyway."

He had brought a cross-cut saw with him and he asked me to take the other end of it and we'd cut it together. So I had my first lesson on the farm.

"Go aisy, now. Just lit the saw go itself and kape it livil."

We soon had it sawn through as it was so rotten. Then Paddy started to split it up into logs, and the children and I stacked them into the turf shed.

In the middle of this work, a tinker woman came down the path from the old road but before she had time to open her mouth, Paddy shouted at her brutally, "Git away outa that! There's nothing fer ye here."

She ran away whimpering and Paddy said, " 'Tis as will fer ye I was here when that one came. She's will known; she'd have ye scalded. 'Tis Bridgie Cran—I put her hoppin'. She'll not trouble ye agin, faith."

As soon as the tree was disposed of, he said he had heard Patsy telling me about the furniture along at the other farm and if I liked we could go along and take a look at it now. As he knew where it was and he also knew the man who had the key, it seemed a good chance to see what was there, so we all went along. There were a few things that we wanted and I asked Paddy how we could bring them back, and he soon solved that problem by heaving a heavy table up on to his back—I was flabbergasted! He told us that we could bring the light stuff and we all set off, laden with furniture, to walk the mile back home through the fields.

After tea Paddy left, and I was just thinking of the kindness of everyone when I saw another visitor coming up from the road below. It was one of Patsy's friends whom we met in the hotel. His arms were full of things he thought we might need. There was coffee, bread, honey, paraffin oil, mirrors covered in beer advertisements, ash-trays, taken from the various hotels, a pack of cards and a newspaper called *The Kerryman*.

He sat and talked till midnight telling me all about Kenmare and everyone in it; I was never more interested in anything.

7 PADDY

PADDY came up every day and there were always
plenty of jobs for him to do. He employed himself—I
never asked him to do anything because I had no
idea what had to be done. He took it upon himself to
run the farm because, he said:

"Ye'll niver deal with the blagarding Irish—ye're
too innocent-looking. They'd have iverything whipped
on ye."

As we hadn't anything to take, his protection wasn't
much use and as for the blagarding Irish—I hadn't
come across any so far, but his help on the farm we
coudn't possibly have done without. Also, he told me
who everyone was, because no one ever said who they
were, so he was our interpreter.

I couldn't understand either the accent or what I
was expected to do; it was all so different from
England, we might have been a million miles away.

I couldn't pay Paddy because we were living on
only the £4 a week from our house in England. If
there was any money left over at the end of the month,
I gave it to him but there hardly ever was. Living was
cheap at that time and we were allowed the farm rent
free, so we just about managed.

Paddy was twenty-eight and had a wife and six or
seven children and lived at the back of Main Street
in Kenmare. He looked like a Dane, muscular and
tall with fair hair and blue eyes. He had a strong
square-jawed face and walked proudly with his head

in the air. His chest and arms were covered in tattoo.
His shirt was always open to the waist, even in the
cold weather. His wife, Nell, was small, dark and
gentle. We always had to go and have a cup of tea
with her if we were in town.

All the children in the street played on their garden
plot in front of the house. It was at one time grass and
flowers, Nell told me, but now it was bare and trodden
iron-hard and covered with rubbish and children's
playthings, plus Paddy's things: sacks, logs, bicycle
parts and so forth.

As soon as we turned the corner into his lane, he
would let out a roar like a lion and the children in
a second would scatter in every direction, leaving the
plot completely deserted for him to walk into his house
like a young lord.

Once in the house, he'd drop his proud manner and
take the latest baby from Nell—who was always
sitting by the fire nursing it—and tell her to 'wet the
tay'. Invariably they would be out of milk or sugar
and Paddy would go off to the shops with the tiny
baby sitting upright in the crook of his arm. I've never
seen a baby look more smug or more comfortable.

Then, while we were drinking the tea, his children
would come creeping shyly back, only to be teased
by Paddy until they were hot with embarrassment
because I was there. "Show Harry yer little piece of
bacon," he'd say to Shawneen, pulling back his short
pants. They would look at him with big, scared eyes,
wondering what he was going to say next. He could
always rely on the baby for a good laugh; he'd present
it with one of his not-too-clean nipples and the baby
would go for it greedily. Then, realizing its mistake,
it would tear its mouth away with a scream, its face

going red and its features wrinkling up like an old man's.

From every dark corner in Paddy's house peered the frightened eyes of his dogs. He loved dogs, whatever shape or breed, and, as it would have been impossible to pay for all their licences, they were trained to lie hidden from the Guards.

His greatest pleasure was to go hunting in the mountains with them. He would stand on top of the Bell Height and whistle a certain whistle which every dog in the town knew, and if any of the others wanted to go with him, the better he liked it. He spent whole days on the mountains, but apart from the rabbits he caught, these expeditions were lucrative in other ways. If any of the people living in remote parts wanted to get married, they asked Paddy to find them a suitable partner, as he knew everyone for miles around, and if these matches were a success, which they usually were, he would be rewarded well for his trouble.

To get back to Paddy's house. It had three rooms, a big stone-flagged Van Gogh-like kitchen with green-painted stairs and banisters leading up to Paddy's room where he and all the boys slept. This room was also used to store potatoes; they covered the floor a foot deep. How they managed to reach their beds through them, I don't know.

Next to it was Nell's room where she and all the girls slept.

8 FOUR VISITORS

EACH day brought more visitors, curious to see the
"foreign woman" and her children, who had come to
live on Bridie's farm at Killah. Paddy had to tell me
who everyone was because everyone always took it
for granted I knew their names and all about them.
The day after Mrs Sullivan brought the hens, our
neighbour from the other side came down bringing a
huge lump of butter she had just churned, wrapped
in a snowy white serviette. She was wearing the same
traditional Irish clothes as Mrs Sullivan: black shawl,
long black skirt, hand-knitted stockings and stout
boots, but whereas Mrs Sullivan didn't care a damn
about what she wore, Mrs Doyle was self-consciously
proud of them. She had been a school teacher, she told
me, and maybe it was because of this she intellectual-
ised everything, her clothes, her religion, and the
customs of the Irish people. She related Irish history,
which I was quite ignorant about, but she made me
interested to learn more. How totally different were
my two neighbours!

Later in the day a girl of about eighteen came, bringing me a large bottle of milk, with a cork in it made
from a cut potato. She immediately took off her coat
and said she would show me how to make soda bread
in the pot oven. As soon as it was cooked we all sat
down to a meal. I fried some eggs—the first ones from
our own hens—and I put a dish of watercress on the

37

table, having found a spring well with watercress growing in it. Although I gave her a knife and fork she preferred to eat everything with her fingers, and did it so deftly she made me feel clumsy with my fork. I surprised her when I began to eat the watercress.

"Sweet Jesus!" she said, horrified, "what arou atin' at all?"

We persuaded her to try a little and her reactions were so violent after nibbling a tiny leaf I was sorry I had told her to try it. She rushed out of the door and after heaving and almost vomiting she came back into the house.

"It have a wild taste, faith," she said, looking shaken. " 'Tis only fit fer messin' th' animals."

We all laughed. "I'll never again eat that trash, yerra," she said, laughing too.

After this girl had gone we noticed a black speck bobbing about on the mountain at the back of the house and as it came nearer we saw that it was a woman. She was leaping about like a child playing, disappearing, and reappearing again behind walls and rocks, and leaping over what must have been bog-water. The next thing she was vaulting the wall into our fields and coming towards the house. She dipped down the bank to the stream and never reappeared so we thought we had seen the last of her, but about half an hour after, she was standing outside the cow-house. I went out to her, and lifting up her heavy black skirt and thrusting her hand into a pocket that stretched right across the front of her green petticoat, she said:

" 'Tis great sport catchin' fishes."

I was waiting to see 'the catch' but instead she brought out an enormous white egg.

"Will ye take a goose's igg, Ma'am?" she said, handing it to me.

She must have seen my look of astonishment because she went on:

" 'Tis quite frish, faith! Ye can put it under a hin or ate it yerself, 'tis aqual to ye!"

I asked her in for a cup of tea and she immediately started to tell me about her troubles.

" 'Tis a show I am, in th'ould rags. If I put a foot over the stip, he'd bate the life outa me. I has a good coat up in the loft I go te Mass in but I can't git it, yerra —he has me persecuted, faith. 'Tis woeful trouble I'm in Ma'am. I hasn't aten a crust uf brid or a bit this long while and I was thinkin', Ma'am, that ye would fitch the priest from Kenmare. The craythurs will be all right wit me till ye gits back," she said, looking at the children.

I gave her tea and cut lots of currant bread, thinking she was hungry, but she just went on talking all the time and crumbled slice after slice between her fingers, not eating any. Thank goodness, she forgot about the priest. She stayed for about two hours and I only understood an odd word and an occasional sentence which hardly made sense to me. When she at last got up to leave I went with her up to the old road and on the way past the stream she pointed to a row of speckled trout lying on the grass bank.

"I cot thim fer the craythurs' tay, God bless them! Good-bye now!" she said, leaping over the wall on to the road and ignoring the gate.

I staggered back into the house and sank into a chair and was holding my reeling head in my hands when I was rudely shaken into alertness by the woman again.

" 'Thould brogue have me persecuted rubbin' agin the heel," she said. "Has ye a scrapeen o' tred te pull it tegither, Ma'am, and I won't be botherin' ye agin," she said pulling off a man's boot that resembled a lump of moss-encrusted rock. I found some white thread, which was all I had, and with three stitches she pulled the enormous hole into a lump and putting back her boot she shouted,

"Tanks, tanks, Ma'am. Good-bye now!"

When I told Paddy about her he roared with laughter and said,

"That one is mad out; why did ye encourage her? The nixt time I see her I'll tell her ye have a gun and ye're not safe with it; that ought te keep her away, faith!"

I was wakened before it was daylight by men shouting on the line below. It was fair day in Kenmare and judging by the swearing and cursing, their cattle must have been jumping the walls into our fields. "Will ye kape te the road, bad cess te ye!" someone shouted and at the same time a loud hammering came on the front door. I imagined it was someone to do with the animals and was surprised when I put my head out of the window to see a woman standing there. "Hello, Ma'am," she said when I asked who it was. "I wondered if ye were makin' the tay. I made a fierce drive te git out early te git te the fair and I hadn't time te wet the tay or a bit and I thought ye'd be gittin' the craythurs off te school and I could have a cup with thim, Ma'am."

The children had a holiday on fair days but I got up all the same and made tea. She washed down a slice of bread with it and crossing herself rose to go, saying :

"I'll not delay, Ma'am. I has te be to and hither before noon. On my hither journey I'll bring ye a bag u' Macroom oatmale fer when ye're short uf colourin'."

That was the first time I had entertained at six o'clock in the morning. But why not, faith!

ONE day when Paddy was out hunting in the mountains, he went into a pub at Lauraugh and who should he see sitting there drinking but Sticks, the children's uncle, and they soon got into conversation.

"What class of a woman is the one back in Bridie's house at Killah?" Sticks began. "Or maybe ye don't know her at all?"

"Lave me alone! Don't I work there?"

"If she's of similar breed to that Patsy one, I would be laving her alone entirely."

"Not at all! she's a dacent woman, faith."

"I suppose ye've heard she's come from over, so's the children can live wit her?"

"I have of course."

"And would ye be advisin' me te let thim go?"

"Why not ye lit thim? They'll be all right with her and amn't I there most days and wouldn't I know soon enough if inything was wrong?"

Two days after this meeting, Stella and Joey burst into my room very early in the morning, shouting: "Get up, Harry, quick! There's a car stopped at the gate below and hundreds of people are getting out and coming up the path."

Three people were coming up the path and another was standing by the car. I dressed quickly while the children ran from room to room so that they wouldn't lose sight of the visitors for one moment. I had just lit a fire and was putting the kettle on when Sticks, followed by Mary and Timmy, pushed open the front door.

"Hullo te ye!" he shouted. "I made free wit the mornin' te bring the craythurs over te ye. 'Tis in a pashtin' hurry I am te git back te the posht. I'll take the tay if ye're makin' it, thin I'll be off." As he washed down bread and tea, she said:

"'Tis perished we are wit the cold in Jimeen's car. We had a right te have waited fer the Mail-car but 'tis pressed fer time I am. They don't know at the Posht Office that I'm here at all, so 'tis off I'll be now," he said, wiping his mouth with the back of his hand, crossing himself and going to the door. Then he turned back and said to Mary and Timmy,

"Ye'll be good craythurs and ye'll not be bold and ye'll help the Missus all ye can?"

"We will," they both said, shyly flushing with their heads down.

"And Timmy—ye'll git the kippins and the bruss in fer kindlin' the fire in the mornin's?"

"I will," he whispered.

"And ye'll wipe the delph, Mary?"

"I will," she said, almost inaudibly.

"And ye'll do as the Missus tells ye?" he said, addressing both of them.

They looked at their feet and swayed about awkwardly without answering.

"Ah, ye will, ye will, ye will, shure. Good-bye now and good luck and I'll be over agin Sunday if I can git a bike," and he was gone.

Stella and Joey stood staring at Mary and Timmy, then Joey went timidly up to Mary and touched her on the arm and said, "Cot". Mary touched her back very shyly and said. "Cot". Stella, seeing the success of this move, went up to Timmy and touched him and said, "Cot". He looked up at her as though he was going to cry but instead he touched her lightly and said "Cot". Slowly the impetus of the game grew until all four were darting about like flies in the air, and saying, "Cot" whenever they bumped one another, and running out into the fields with the same game. I heard only the word "Cot" for the next hour.

I called them in for a meal, thinking that a good deal of their shyness would be gone after their long game, but how mistaken I was! I asked them if they had had any breakfast and they looked at me and their lips moved but no sound came—fear throttled their voices! After this, I thought it would be kinder if I didn't speak to them at all and left everything to Stella and Joey who were laughing all the time—both at them and with them, because they couldn't show their delight in any other way. After Stella and Joey had eaten their fill, and Mary and Timmy not a bite, they all went into the fields again, but my two made all the noise.

I thought that maybe they would feel less shy if I suggested that they should all carry water in from the stream for their baths. This proved to be a successful move. The more they swilled the water over the top of their buckets the merrier they became—the floor was like a lake before long, but what did it matter?— it could be broomed out of the front door in a minute and I had a huge log fire burning; it would soon dry up.

Stella and I lifted the zinc bath up by the handles on to the stones at either side of the fire and as soon as it was hot enough, Stella shouted, "Bags first," which was just as well because Mary and Timmy could go last and know what they had to do. Joey followed in Stella's water, then we tipped it out of the front door and watched it run away down the fields. We filled the bath up again with clean water and when it was all ready for them to step into, they were too scared to do so.

"Just try your toe in it first," Stella said, roaring with laughter. After some time Mary stood up in the water and it took about another quarter of an hour to persuade her to sit down in it.

"Have you never had a bath before?" Stella said, and Mary shook her head.

A black rim appeared round both of their waists where the water reached up to, and it took several baths before it disappeared for good.

Patsy had brought new pyjamas over from England for them and the next business was to get them into them. They had obviously never seen pyjamas before because they were about to get dressed again to go to bed. Never have I known getting ready for bed to cause such hectic fun! When at last they were in bed, Mary and Timmy gabbled monotonously for such a long time I crept up to ask them why they couldn't sleep and was shocked to see that they were talking in their sleep.

The next morning and every morning for the next few weeks the first thing Joey did on wakening was to shout, "Mary and Timmy!" and two small voices from the next room would answer, "Fwhat?" and Joey would lie down again, satisfied that this wonderful increase in the family hadn't been a dream.

To Stella and Joey it was almost too good to be true to have two more children always there to play with.

10 THE SHEEP DOG

PADDY came up to the house one evening with a pack of mongrels at his heels; he was on his way home after another day's hunting in the mountains.

"Come out here and look at the dog I got for ye," he shouted. " 'Twas tied up in a cabin and it half starving. I gave the fella a packet of cigarettes and he gave me the dog."

"I don't want it. You have it, you like dogs," I said feebly, not wanting to offend him.

" 'Tis a nice dog, and the others would like it; what's more, a dog is useful about the place. She's a thorough-bred collie and her name's Lassie. She's not fully grown yet, but ye can see she's going to be a beauty all the same."

As soon as I showed the first signs of weakening, Paddy was off, and Lassie was ours.

The hen's food—a mixture of potatoes, yellow-meal and buttermilk—was standing on the table, so I put it down on the floor, never expecting her to eat any of it, but she swallowed it down with great gulps until she emptied the bucket, then she went sniffing round looking for more. A box of onions which I intended planting that evening was standing in the corner and she gulped these down too— I was afraid to take them from her—then, with her nose to the ground, she zig-zagged about sniffing for still more. She found some mouldy prunes, which I had thrown out for the hens to pick at, and she swallowed these down whole, too.

In the evening, I was trying to read, but found it almost impossible because Lassie was lying stretched out under the table, and her stomach was making a squealing noise as though she had swallowed a bag of kittens, or else she was jerking violently and letting out little yelps. Then, suddenly, she sat up and let out a piercing howl which sent me jumping to my feet; she rolled over on her side, frothing at the mouth and trembling frantically all over. Then, like a cannon opening fire, all the food she had eaten shot out of her mouth and across the floor. I was terrified, horrified and disgusted. "She's a nice dog" Paddy had said without knowing. Wait till I see him! I quickly went to bed and all through the night I was being wakened by Lassie being sick and having more fits and I thought by the morning she would surely be dead. I couldn't bury her, I thought, I couldn't even go into that room again. Paddy will have to do it. I felt very cross and had no sympathy for the dog at all.

The next morning I went down and as I passed the room I opened the door a tiny crack, just so that I could be still more furious when Paddy came, and I got the shock of my life. The dog leapt at my throat —so I thought—but she was only trying to get out of the room. I opened the back door, weak at the knees with fright, and she leapt out like a greyhound beginning a race and dived into a thicket of brambles and gorse, and, forcing a pathway through it, had one fit followed by another.

Paddy arrived and I told him the whole story. He didn't say a word, only his lips compressed into thin lines and his face flushed, and he got up and marched out to where Lassie was resting after a fit. She looked up at him with fiery, shifty eyes as he thrust his bare arm into the thicket and grabbed her by the rough collar of hair on her neck, and pulled her out squirming and squealing, and, with her wolf's teeth bared in a snarl, he carried her up to the deep pool under the bridge and plunged her in. A struggle ensued between Paddy and the dog and Paddy won—the dog began to drown.

"Let her go, you'll drown her," I shouted.

"That's what I intend," he said looking up at me coldly.

I was shocked. I ran up to him and giving him a big push I shouted, "Stop it, stop it."

He gave me a look of contempt, but let go his grip.

"Nixt time ye can do the job yerself," he said crossly, "because she'll niver pull out of thim fits."

Lassie crept furtively back to her run in the briars, and lay down with her head on her front paws, ready to escape or attack if anyone tried to touch her again.

I put bread and milk in dishes at either side of her run and when no one was looking, she ate it and she never had another fit. After a week she ventured out, but it was another three weeks before she came into the house and still longer before she would allow us to touch her.

She grew to be the best-looking dog in the district. She wasn't very sensible but she was very beautiful, with her snowy collar of hair, as thick as a polar bear's, and her foxy hair and luxuriant tail. Her tawny eyes always seemed to be asking nervously, "What are we going to do now?"

11 CHRISTMAS

MARY and Timmy had never celebrated Christmas before in the usual conventional way. The only thing they had done on Christmas Day was to go to early morning Mass and Patsy had sent them each a present and that was all. So we told them all about it and they got very excited as it was only a few weeks off. They wanted to send everyone they knew a present which they had made themselves and, as none of them had any spare money, they had to make do with what material they could find lying around.

They spent hours on the strand looking for stones to paint. Timmy found one the shape of a motor-car and Stella one that resembled a negro's head. She had great fun painting it black and covering its neck with blobs of coloured paint for beads—even its hair was a mass of curls formed in the stone. Joey found dozens of dogs' heads and she painted them white with black spots and coloured collars. Mary found one the shape of a duck with its beak resting on its back. Timmy found pieces of wood and with his pen-knife carved plates, blocky egg-cups and toasting forks. Mary knitted things with scraps of wool and Stella painted pictures and Christmas cards—they all made cards but Stella's were outstanding, so she gave all the others advice.

Joey, after hearing everyone spell out 'To' and 'From', which they wrote inside their cards, boasted to me, "I know how to spell 'From'".

49

"Go on! You don't!"

"I do. T-O!" she said proudly.

When I was in town the woman in the shop where we dealt told me that the pig lorry was going to Tralee the next day and if I would like to go I could have a seat beside the driver—I'd be able to see more of the country. I was delighted to go because at the same time I could buy a few Christmas presents for the children—there was nothing in Kenmare. So I was up early and cycled into town before anyone was up.

We set off with a load of squealing pigs behind us and climbed for miles and miles up the mountains until we reached Moll's Gap, then we turned to make the descent into Killarney. Behind us lay the Black Valley, where the sun never penetrated. Ahead the road wound its way down through boulders and rocks, and as we got lower, grass and heather began to appear, then more luxuriant growth such as arbutus trees, pines, silver birch, and holly. I had always thought of just "holly"—never of being separate trees like the ones here, which might have been growing beside the Parthenon they looked so classical with their sturdy, silvery-pink trunks and their olive-green foliage. As we got lower still, we saw the Killarney lakes stretched out in a long line below us. The lake water was deep violet and the mountains were reflected in its glassy surface. Deer standing shoulder deep in rusty bracken were looking at us and a red fox ran leisurely across the road. Then we were running level and the road ran so close to the lake we could hear the water clapping up against the smooth black rocks. Then along the Muckross road into the town of Killarney and on through the Vale of

Tralee—which wasn't as beautiful as the song makes
out—not after the Kenmare-Killarney road.

I was given only half an hour in Tralee before the
lorry returned but I was lucky in finding shops which
sold all sorts of exciting things. I bought wooden
hoops, hurling sticks, bouncing balls, playing cards,
depicting Irish kings and queens, crayons, sweets
called 'Pegs Legtops', whips, tops, skipping-ropes,
books, coloured glass alleys and marbles. The pigs
were left to be made into bacon and we roared home
in an empty lorry. I left all the presents in the shop
in Kenmare so that the children wouldn't see them,
and cycled home feeling quite anxious because I had
left them for so long, but I need not have worried as
they were still absorbed in making presents, and were
covered from head to foot in paint.

All the Kenmare shops gave their customers Christmas presents, and while I had been away, 'The
Dummy'—a deaf and dumb boy who worked in the
shop—had been up and left a large box. We opened it
up and on the top lay a bright blue candle two feet
long, and underneath, a Christmas cake and pudding,
tinned fruit, preserves, biscuits, chocolates and nuts.

Christmas came at last and the children went to
bed pent up with excitement. I waited until they were
asleep, then spent the next few hours parcelling up
their toys, filling their stockings, and decorating a
Christmas tree, which I had kept as a secret.

It was after midnight when I finished. I opened the
front door and stood looking out across the sea at all
the houses twinkling like stars with their Christmas
candles burning in the windows. The Holy Family
were abroad on Christmas Eve and the candles burnt
all through the night to show them where they might

rest. All the houses had been newly lime-washed for this occasion too.

The night was warm and misty, and although it was unseasonable weather, I never felt Christmas more near. A donkey brayed in the far distance and was answered by another near by. They sounded like souls in agony in a pristine world—the atmosphere felt close to the Bible.

The children were up at six o'clock tearing open their parcels and eating whatever sweets they found and unable to concentrate on any one toy for longer than a second.

Some children from the farms along the old road called down to them to come to Mass and they all went off, Stella and Joey too. They came back bringing five of the Barry children from the farm beyond Sullivan's. I had never before seen children with such wild, innocent faces—untouched by puritanism. Their hair was in a ravel of wisps and curls and they were wearing tweed dresses—obviously cut down from their parents' coats—which reached down to their bare feet. They played in the stream, letting their dresses seep up the water.

In the evening we went along to their house and danced in the kitchen to old gramophone records of Irish reels. The baby had a special dance of her own; she bobbed up and down in her long nightdress to the "tick-tick" of the milk separator.

The next day was St Stephen's Day and the "Wren Boys" came with blackened faces and a few old rags on for disguise; they held a decorated holly branch with a stuffed wren tied in the middle of it, and asked for pennies to "bury the wrin", then half-recited, half-sang:

The Wrin, the wran, the king of all birds,
On St Stephen's Day was cot in the furze,
Although he be little, his family be great,
So put on the kittle and give us a trate . . .

We ran out of pennies long before midday, when they were supposed to stop.

Paddy came along in the afternoon and suggested cycling to the races at Kilgarvan. We arrived to find a race in progress; the jockeys were the local boys riding their own ponies and horses and all the onlookers were running along the field, shouting madly and trying to keep pace with the horses.

The moon was up when Paddy and I were cycling home and the sound of melodeon music floated out of the open doors of every house, pub and dance-hall. Christmas was over but the thrill of living in Ireland was still going on.

12 THE GOAT AND KID

"I JUST heard tell passing up through the town this morning, of a goat and kid sellin' back at Dromuckity, by the Sullivan fella. He only wants fourteen shillin's for the two of thim, so I told him we'd take a look at thim this avining," Paddy announced as soon as he arrived one morning.

"Don't be crazy! What do we want with a goat and kid?" I said.

"Ye need the milk, don't ye?"

"We do, but not goat's milk. Ugh! I couldn't bear it."

"Inyway, there's no harm done looking at thim, and they're asy to manage. Ye can learn to milk a goat, then perhaps ye could buy a cow later on."

That evening, Paddy and I set off with a rope 'just in case', we climbed the mountain at the back of the house until we were able to look down on to Dromuckity valley with the broad pewter-coloured river winding down to meet the sea. Then we bounded down the heathery slopes, jumping over rocks and bog-water after crossing the river at the foot of the mountains, and we climbed up fields at the other side to Sullivan's house. The goats were on the mountain somewhere, so we all went out to 'take a look at them'. As we walked along, the 'Sullivan fella' told us that his sister had won the goat—which was in kid—at a whist drive, and that it was a great pet of hers. He boosted them up so much that I couldn't think why he wanted to sell them. Doll and Nancy were their names, and they were both pure white, with amber-coloured eyes flecked with brown. It didn't take Paddy long, when he saw how impressed I was, to put the rope round Doll's horns and hand over the fourteen shillings.

"We'll milk her in turns," Mary shouted to the others as they all raced up the fields to meet us, but they little knew what they were in for.

Stella was the first to try, and she found it almost impossible, because the goat refused to stand still; Mary had to sit on her back while Timmy held her beard with both hands and Joey her tail; but even with everyone's help she still managed to evade the milker. Paddy fettered her two legs to prevent her from going home and all that evening and every minute of the days to come, the goat gazed towards her beloved mountains, bleating continuously. The kid didn't mind so long as her mother was there, and so long as it could squeeze through gaps in the hedge and eat the young lettuce plants. I hated both of them. And I hated the deathly white milk Doll reluctantly gave us. Then one day the fetter snapped and I watched Doll rock up the fields as fast as she could with Nancy bleating at her heels, scramble over the wall and make off towards the Dromuckity mountains.

"Thank God," I said aloud, "I never want to see either of you again."

As soon as Paddy heard about it he wanted to go and fetch them back straight away, but this time I just flatly refused. A week passed by, and I had almost forgotten that we had ever owned goats, when I was rudely reminded. As I was cycling into Kenmare, a horse and car passed me, and the driver, seeing who I was, pulled his horse to a stop and jumped off his car.

"So 'tis ye, Ma'am," he said angrily, "tell me, why hasn't ye been te fitch yer goats?"

"I don't want them back," I answered weakly.

"Then Ma'am, ye'll have to dispose of them in the proper manner. Hasn't they eaten a field o' cabbage by me, and I'm thinking, Ma'am, 'tis ye will have te pay fer the damage," he said flatly, jumping back on to his seat on the car and lashing his horse to a gallop. 'Paddy and his blasted goats,' I thought, 'he'll have to get me out of this somehow.'

That evening someone knocked loudly on the front door, and there stood a boy who looked like a messenger from out of the Bible. He had a head of dark curls and a pink angelic face. He was dressed in rags and held a long, shepherd's crooked stick. But my admiration turned to fright when I heard what he had to say.

"There's a goat and a kid on my mountain, and I hear they belong to ye, Ma'am."

"Oh, yes, maybe they do," I said timidly.

"I was wondering would ye think of selling? If so, I would give ye the price ye paid fer thim." Could I trust my own ears—or was I dreaming? I didn't waste any time bargaining with him in case he changed his mind; he gave me the fourteen shillings saying:

"I hope ye're satisfied, Ma'am." Satisfied! I would have *given* them to him for *nothing* if he had asked me.

Some weeks passed and I saw the boy again; he was standing in a shop doorway in Kenmare, looking very glum.

"Hello!" I said cheerily, "how are the goats?"

"Did, Ma'am."

"Dead! What d'you mean? How can they be dead?"

"They got clifted, the two of thim, but the kid's alive."

"What's 'clifted' mean?"

"They fell off-of a cliff."

I felt I was somehow to blame, and thought I ought to give him his money back.

That same evening Carmel Conner came to see us. She lived near the Sullivans and knew the entire history of the goats. Evidently the wild billy-goats lived up on the heights and never came down to the lower slopes unless they were in search of a she-goat, and this had happened to Nancy; she was being courted by a wild billy. All three of them had broken into a field of cabbages and eaten it entirely bare; Carmel had seen them after this, 'fat out after the cabbages', and they were all three making their way up the mountain again. There was a fierce feud going on between the Sullivans and their neighbour, because the neighbour's children were blamed for stoning the goat to death when she was 'clifted'.

Months later, Mary came running in from school to say she had just seen the goats in a field; she *knew* they were our goats.

But by this time I couldn't have cared less.

13 THE COW

THE children came running down the fields, tumbling over one another to get into the house first. I hadn't expected to see them for another hour, as they usually dawdled in the town for a long time after school was over. They all started gabbling at once.

"What's the matter? What's happened?" I asked. "Only one of you speak at a time."

"A man stopped us as we were coming through the town," Stella began.

"He looked like a tinker," Timmy interrupted.

"He wasn't a tinker because he knew our names," Mary said impatiently.

"He asked us 'did we want a cow?'" they all said at once.

"You're talking nonsense; no one is going to *give* us a cow."

"Only for the winter," Mary went on.

"Not even for the winter—not when milk is so scarce," I said.

"He said he was going to bring it along this evening," Timmy said, almost in tears because I wouldn't believe them. They had seen Paddy in the town, and he'd promised to come up. 'Thank God for that anyway,' I thought, 'he'll deal with this madman with the cow,' still thinking there must be some mistake.

We were sitting at the kitchen table eating our dinner, and suddenly I stopped in astonishment with my fork loaded with mashed potatoes half-way to my

mouth. I saw a man pass the window followed by a
taut rope which I thought was never going to end, then
a black cow filled the window space. I went to the
door and was addressed by a tall straggly man in
what seemed to me to be Gaelic; as he spoke he frothed
at the mouth while one eye looked up and the other on
the ground. In the middle of our muddle of conversation Paddy rounded the corner and as I couldn't understand either of them, I went in to finish my dinner.
Through the open doorway I saw the rope being thrust
into Paddy's hand and the man leaving.

"Well ye have a cow now," Paddy said, smiling; the
more animals we acquired the better he seemed to like
it.

"He couldn't feed her because he hadn't enough hay
to last the winter and seeing all the fine grass here, he
thought that in exchange for the grazing ye could
take what milk she gives, and in the spring he'll take
her back agin."

So it was true. We had a cow and we'd have plenty
of milk for the winter, and we needn't be begging our
neighbours to sell it to us when they hadn't enough
for themselves. I liked the look of her too; she wasn't a
tame old cow but a wild animal, a black Polly, Kerry
cow with long legs. I asked Timmy the Irish for 'wild',
and he told me it was 'Fian', so I called her Fian immediately.

Paddy led her into the haggard, then he blocked the
gap into it with a mass of blackthorn branches which
he cut from a nearby tree. Her eyes seemed to be
smoking an evil blue-brown, then suddenly with a leap
like a deer's, she sprang through the thorny mass of
branches and galloped off across the field. Paddy ran
after her and caught her just before she reached the

old road and he called to us to fetch him a rope to fetter her. A thorn had pierced into the pupil of one of her eyes and tears were rolling down her face. After a good deal of trouble Paddy managed to pull it out, then he sent one of the children back to the house for a bucket, and milked her there and then, sitting in the field.

"Lard God! Ye'll niver pull the milk outa this one," he said, pushing his head into her side and using all the force he had in his fingers. "She's the toughest cow I've iver handled. No wonder yer man wanted to be shot uf her."

For the next three days Paddy milked her, then to my astonishment he announced, "From this off, ye'll have to milk her yerself and if ye can't manage it, thin ye don't deserve a cow at all."

I nearly didn't deserve a cow at all. It took me hours to drag a few drops from her.

I milked her in whatever field she happened to be and it was just as well I wasn't in the cow-house; the field gave me plenty of space to be kicked around in. She swished her tail in my face and she wrenched the hair-clips out of my hair until the tuft on the end of her tail was like a prickly pear. She kicked the bucket from between my knees and sent me rolling over and she'd walk off leaving me sitting on the three-legged stool in the middle of the field. I tried singing to her, having heard that this was the thing to do, but she must have disliked my songs. I would lose my temper and yell at her, "Keep your precious milk, you nasty, tough thing—I wouldn't have it if it poured out of you", and she would walk off, well able to keep the tiny amount of milk she was carrying.

As time went on I improved, but she didn't; she

remained tough and that wasn't her only fault either!
She was a thief. She preferred the grass on other
people's land to ours and being agile, she was able to
leap over any wall. The first time she went thieving,
I found her over in Doyle's.

"Git outa that, ye thavin' bashtard," Jim Doyle was
shouting at her and whacking her over the back. I
was horrified.

"You'll hurt her, don't" I shouted.

"Hurt her is it! Doesn't she deserve all that's
comin' to her and she thavin' my grass?"

But there's grass everywhere, I thought. He must
be mad, but I soon learned how precious grass was.

14 THE COCK AND HENS

It was cold and damp out of doors so the children were playing in the kitchen cutting out horses and cars and painting them. As soon as they finished they would drive them into town, using all the abusive language they could lay tongue to. I was making a basket out of palm leaves—I'd learned how to make them from the Irish Countrywoman's Association which I attended every week in the Carnegie Hall. We were all so absorbed that we got a shock when we heard loud banging on the back door. "Tinkers, tinkers!" each one of the children said, dropping their horses and running up the stairs. Their fear was infectious; I opened the door and stood there petrified, staring straight into the face of a tall thin woman.

They've come for me, I thought. She had grey hair and grey bristles growing out of her chin and even her complexion was ashen. Her cold steely eyes were fixed on mine with an expression that said, 'When you're ready'. I was rooted to the spot and my mind was blank. We must have looked like two cocks about to fight. After what seemed eternity, she made a step towards me and I quickly stepped back and we stood looking at one another again. Then, without any more nonsense, she pushed past me and walked into the kitchen and sat herself down on the seat. Looking up at all the frightened faces peeping through the banisters, she said, "Hello, Mary,"—she knows Mary!—the tension collapsed. I thought what a fool I'd made of myself and how rude I had been not to have asked her in.

"Come down te me till I show yez what I have fer ye in the bag," she said to the children.

They came scrambling down as she was untying the piece of rope round the top of it. As soon as it was open, a huge cock jumped out on to the seat, then down on to the floor and, shaking off the humiliation of the sack, it let out an ear-splitting "Cock-a-doodle-do" and strutted to the open door where it took wing, rising and falling over the boundary walls in Doyle's land until it disappeared out of sight. The children gave chase but came back without having seen it.

"He'll be back te ye," the woman said, laughing hysterically.

She was right! After three days, Jim Doyle called to the children to come and get our cock; it was up there with his hens. They carried him down and put him in the middle of a bunch of hens and he stepped with dignity among them with his tail feathers stiffly arched and quivering.

It didn't take him long to become their lord and master. He flew up on to the hawthorn tree to roost that same evening followed by the six hens and from that day to this the hen-house was ignored entirely— even when the hens had chickens they still roosted up the hawthorn tree, leaving them cheeping below and trying to jump up to their mothers. They had to squeeze into cracks in the walls or in any cranny they could find. No rat ever took them and they all survived and, like their parents, roosted on the tree when they were old enough to fly up on to it.

We soon got to know all the idiosyncrasies of these six hens and that one cock. Never having had anything to do with hens before, I watched them with interest, and discovered that far from being 'too stupid to run out of the rain', they were clever, wily and even humorous, and each one possessed an individual character of its own.

To mention four: there was a plain white hen which we named 'Silvia'; she was emancipated! Free to be as unhen-like as she chose. Every morning she would be waiting at the back door, ready to nip in sideways as soon as it was opened. Once in she could drop her skittish manner and strut with dignity around the kitchen, singing "Caw Caw", curling up her claws with deliberation before each step and jerking her feathery neck this way and that, and stretching it to twice its normal length to look up on to the seat. There was usually one of the children's vests there, a jersey or a coat flung down—this was what she was looking for. She would jump up and pick it up with her beak and give it a sharp kick backwards, just to test its pliability, then the business of making her nest would begin—this took sometimes a whole hour. She tweeked the cloth with her beak, kicked it about with first one claw then the other, and shuffled it into shape with her body. With fierce yellow startled eyes she would view her work and come to the conclusion it was far from perfect and the whole performance would be gone through again. When she sat down she still wasn't satisfied; she would twist her head, first right, then left and tweek at the material fussily. Then she'd get up and face in the opposite direction two or three times. When she was finally satisfied, she would sit unblinkingly to await the journey of the egg. As soon as the time came she would quickly stand up and putting her head between her legs, watch the egg slide out.

Once it was laid she had no further interest—in fact, she couldn't get away quick enough. She would jump down and run out of the door cackling loudly and the cock with mighty strides would join her and they'd both go off together cackling loudly for the next five minutes. The cock took part of the credit, imitating her cackle exactly.

Another hen we named 'Veronica Lake'. She was a small, black Minorca with a white tuft of feathers growing out of the top of her head and a comb which fell over one eye. She was a born actress! She knew exactly the time when we would be having breakfast and she'd jump up on to the outside window-sill and go through her varied repertoire—she could reach amazingly high notes, holding and lengthening her 'Caw-Caws' at will. She was always a success: we always laughed.

Then there was the big, brown, fat, motherly hen. We just called her 'The Broody Hen' because that was her entire character—she'd do nothing else but sit on eggs. People used to come for miles to borrow her because she was such a good sitter and never deserted her nest.

But the 'Speckeldy Hen' was the cleverest and the most wily. I often pitted my wits against hers and she always won. She laid away like the others but she'd go so much further afield and it was impossible to find her nest, and even though I would run to the place where she started her cackle and beat around the growth with a stick, her nest always eluded me.

All the hens were bringing twelve and sometimes fifteen chickens cheeping to the back door for food, until we had so many I couldn't count them, so I made up my mind that they weren't going to hatch out any more. The Speckeldy Hen was laying over in Doyle's land and although I spent hours searching for her nest, I couldn't find it. Then I had an idea how to fool her. I put one of the children's green oilskin mackintosh capes over my head and looking out of a buttonhole, I sat over in the field with my back against a rock. I hadn't to wait long; over she came but she took her time. She caw-cawed looking from side to side, picking up bits here and there—no one would ever have known that she had a nest in the vicinity. She came right up to me I hardly dared breathe. I was watching her so acutely I never heard a cow come up to me until I felt a blast of hot breath fill the cape. I leapt to my feet and of course frightened away the hen. When I came back to the house, there she was sitting under the monkey puzzle tree with several others, pecking fleas from between her feathers as though she didn't know what a nest was.

The next day I tried again. Fixing the cape over my head when I was in the field, I settled down on my haunches, imagining I was exactly like a rock, to await the speckled hen. Over she came and went through the same pottering performance and just as I thought to myself, this time you've had it old girl! a voice above me shouted:

"What arou doing at all?" I jumped up pulling the cape off my head, to see Mrs Doyle standing there. She had watched me from her house above and thought I had taken leave of my senses—I noticed she had a big stick in her hand just in case . . .

I explained and she said indignantly, "I've never been bet by a hen yet," and she started to pull away the growth from the bottom of the hedge and beat about in the long reeds but after half an hour or so she had to give it up. When Murty Sullivan heard about it, he laughed, " 'Tis asy out, yerra, I'll have it found in liss than a minute." He tried but he had to give up too. After a few weeks, the Speckeldy Hen brought fourteen yellow fluff balls cheeping to the back door for food. Weeks later I found her nest in the middle of a patch of green reeds. Brown reeds mixed with feathers in a perfect circle formed the nest. They were beginning to make nests like wild birds!

15 SCHOOL

"WHY can't I go to school?" Joey cried every morning as she watched Stella, Mary and Timmy running down the fields with their satchels on their backs and their hoops over their arms. She wore me down in the end and, although she was only five, I let her go, knowing she was too young to walk the two miles into Kenmare, and then back again in the evenings, but as she was so set on going, I thought she could try it anyway. The three who went to school grew tired of the wooden hoops I had brought back from Tralee and had found old bicycle wheels instead, like those the Kenmare children played with, and like them, they called them 'Bowlies'. These bowlies they kept hidden in the high ferns at the gate on the Line—the road below—to avoid the bother of bringing them up to the house each day. As soon as they reached the road, these bowlies became their horses. Joey joined them at this time and as she had no bowlie, they told her that she could be a foal and run behind. They set off, lashing their horses with sticks, and shouting them on to greater and greater speed. Poor Joey was a fat podge and they were out of sight in no time. She ploughed along as fast as she could and caught up with them at the 'skeeting rock'. This was a huge sloping rock on the strand, and every day they stopped to play at sliding down it. But no sooner was she there than they ran on to their next stopping-place, which was the arched bridge spanning the sea inlet. Here, their game

was to run up the arches to see if they could reach
the top. If they had fallen, they would have crashed
sixty feet to the sea-weed covered rocks and water
below. Again Joey would catch up with them only to
see them packing up that game and running off,
swearing and lashing at their horses, over the Bell
Height to Shelbourne Street, where Timmy turned
off to the boys' school, while the other two flew on
through the town and through the big gates of the
convent.

If they got there early enough—which they made
a point of doing—they were given yellow-meal stirabout which the nuns provided for the country children who had long journeys to make. Joey arrived at
the convent alone, fretted, hot, and with her heart
pumping against her ribs. On one of these occasions,
she was in such a state, she peed on the floor to the
amusement of all the other children, who immediately
nick-named her 'Piss-a-bed'. They weren't horrible to
her—it was only fun—but Joey hated to be laughed
at.

At lunchtime, the nuns gave a bun to each child as
she left; my lot were supposed to eat their sandwiches
in the Muxna Hotel together with the Muxna children,
and this they did for a week or two, until a woman
who had been a friend of Mary's and Timmy's parents
invited them for a cup of cocoa during the lunch hour.
They were delighted to accept and Joey had just
started school when this arrangement was agreed
upon. They told her she wasn't to tell me because I
might be cross with them for leaving the Hotel. I
did find this out and they had to tell me a little of
what they were up to but they, by no means, told me
all. This is what happened:

I was in Kenmare one day round about their lunch hour, so I thought I would go to the convent to see them as they came out. I was standing at the gates when the school doors burst open and the children poured out into the yard and ran, screaming and shouting, in every direction. Stella came tumbling out of the door employing her two hands to put on her coat and with a bun clenched between her teeth. I waited, thinking how pleased and surprised she would be to see me but she raced past. I shouted "Stella!" but she ran on having neither seen nor heard me. Never mind, I thought, I'll wait for Mary and Joey. They were coming now, both with buns in their teeth. Mary was struggling to get her coat on as she ran, and trying to shake off Joey's tight grip on it. I tried to grab them as they ran past, but there were so many other children all at the gate at the same time I couldn't catch them.

Mary sped along the road like the White Queen, with Joey hanging on to her coat; they went so fast Joey seemed to be floating. I wondered why all the hurry? and thought I'll see them at the hotel anyway. but was surprised to see them turn a corner into a side street. I reached the corner in time to see them disappearing into a strange house, so I walked away, puzzling over their behaviour. When they came home that evening, I asked them what they'd been up to. They looked evasively from one to the other, and Stella said:

"Oh, just to have a cup of cocoa with a woman who knows Mary and Timmy." Things were becoming more and more of a mystery. Sometimes they would come home and refusing to eat their dinner, they would flop on their beds and say they 'felt awful'. How could they, I wondered, on a few lettuce sandwiches and an apple? Then a further clue came my way.

I was looking into a gorse bush where I had heard scuffling, wondering if it was a rabbit, and what should I see but all their packages of sandwiches, and a huge rat devouring them. This they found hard to explain away. They said they put them there intending to pick them up later because someone had asked them to go for something to eat at lunch hour. Then, after a few weeks, Joey became very ill and it was then that the whole story came out. The woman in the house in the side street had given them, not only a cup of cocoa, but huge meals of anything the family was having, such as liver and bacon, crubeens (pig's feet), black puddings and the like. This meant that they had breakfast at home, stirabout when they arrived at the convent, a bun at lunch hour, a full course meal and their own sandwiches, when they hadn't stuffed them into a gorse bush, plus several ice-creams which they bought with the odd pennies people were forever giving them, and anything that was growing by the roadside on the way home, such as 'huts' (blaeberries) sorrel leaves, sloes, wild strawberries, and so forth. Mary became rotund, Timmy and Stella looked very run-down and they caught colds, while Joey gave up the ghost altogether and went to bed with a temperature of a hundred and one.

After three weeks, I carried Joey—a light little bundle in a blanket—downstairs, and propped her up on the seat in front of the kitchen fire, while I wrote to the nuns to tell them that she would not be returning to the convent, as I intended sending her to Dourus School, where the children were more of her own age.

It was March 17th, St Patrick's Day and the day when everyone 'put down' their potatoes.

Paddy told me that potatoes were the most important of all the crops and that we would have to grow them, so we had been preparing for this day for the past month or more. First of all we selected a field out of the twenty-six acres to make into a potato garden, then we sent to Dublin for special seed. It was worth while trying to grow 'champions', Paddy said, because they were the best of all the varieties, big, flowery, and so rich and yellow that they needed no butter mixed through them. Their only fault was that the seed was running out; they had been going for generations and they were becoming tired and diseased and many of them had black rot in their centres, and as I'd never grown a potato in my life I had to take his word for it.

It was the woman's job to cut the seed, he said, so as soon as they arrived, the milking stool was put outside the back door for me to sit on, a sack was tied round my waist and in one of my hands was placed a potato and in the other a sharp knife, and I was shown how it was done. The top of the potato was called 'the rose' and it was covered in eyes; round the sides there weren't so many eyes, and at the bottom, where the stalk attaching it to the plant had been, there were no eyes at all, so this part was first of all cut away as being no use, except to boil up for the hens' mess. Then out of the medium-sized potatoes that we had, three seeds were cut; each triangular piece had to have two eyes in it—in case one eye was eaten by worms. The cut seed was called 'the skillarn' and the piece that was no use 'the skilloge'. I thought I'd never get the black stain off my fingers. I was at it for three days, until my back ached. The seed then had to be dusted in lime and allowed two or three days to dry out. When I had finished this job I thought I was due for a rest but I found that much heavier work lay ahead. The next thing was to find two horses to do the ploughing, and Paddy spent days trying to get them. Jim Doyle had a horse he would lend all right, but it didn't agree with Sullivan's horse; Barrys were willing to lend their horse, but it got on neither with Sullivan's nor with Doyle's. In the end he did find two horses that were not going to destroy one another. Their owners had to come along too because the horses wouldn't follow anyone else.

Paddy stayed away the day they came to plough because there was nothing for him to do, but I was never busier. When I wasn't feeding the horses with oats, I was feeding the men with bread and tea. All day from the low field near the road, I could hear the plough-men shouting to their horses, "Up on it, git outa that," and without any other orders they knew exactly what to do. The plough turned 'the barn' or top sod over, forming ridges, and the following day, Paddy and I had to hack the clots out of the up-turned soil with a special implement called a 'griofan'. By this time the seed was ready to 'stick'. This was done by thrusting a spade into the soil on the ridge, pressing it forward and dropping the seed into the hole. Then the children came behind 'closing the holes' by banging the earth down again with a spade.

Then came the job of spreading the manure on the ridges and on top of the potatoes. Lime had to be the first layer because it destroyed the other manures if it was put on top of them. So Paddy had to borrow his father's 'jinnet' and car, and fetch a load of lime from the kiln at the other side of Kenmare. There was plenty of lime-stone on the other side of the sea inlet, but none at all on our side. He dumped the car load on the field and the children and I had to carry buckets of water from the stream to slake it, and when it was broken down into powder, we spread it on the ridges. Manure from the cow-house came next. For this Paddy borrowed his father's donkey and 'ciosans'—panniers— and we spent the whole day journeying back and forth, carrying it down to the low field and spreading it on top of the lime. Next came the seaweeds. They had to be cut off the rocks, carted up to the field, dumped in a heap and allowed to rot slightly for two or three days, then spread on top of the manure. Then the plough had to come again to plough up 'the trenches'. This time it took only one horse and plough to loosen the soil, so that Paddy and I could shovel it up on top of all the layers of manure. This done we could rest for a few weeks until the stalk grew to be a foot high, then once again the horse and plough had to come to loosen the soil in the trenches so that we could 'second earth' the growing plants. This was done by shovelling soil up from the ridges round the plants. The final manuring was a sprinkling of 'guano' round each plant. This was a grey powdery stuff we bought in sacks and was made from the excrement of sea-birds.

At this time of the year instead of shouting " 'Tis a fine day, thank God", everyone would say "How's the stalks?" After all that labour, the condition of the potato stalk was one's only concern. Since the famine in Ireland, everyone sprays his potatoes against blight; so when crop grew to be big healthy plants, Paddy filled a container with stream water, mixed copper sulphate in it and walked up and down the ridges spraying blue liquid on to all the leaves of the plant. Our potatoes grew to be as healthy as anyone else's and our hens hadn't died—I was rapidly becoming a farmer.

The new potatoes were lifted without any trouble and so were the second earlies, but the main crop had to be lifted in September, selected, so that no bad one was among them to spread disease to the others, and stored in pits. These were made on the field itself by digging a hole like a grave, lining it with straw, throwing in the potatoes, covering them with straw, then fine soil, roof-shaped and perfectly symmetrical. Rats would often get into these pits and destroy a large percentage of the crop.

How potatoes can be so cheap I don't know after all the work and worry they entail.

It is far from a happy crop; so many things can go wrong; apart from the blight and the rats, the weather, if too wet, turns them black and if too dry, produces scab or restricts growth. Why, I wonder, has it become the most important crop on the farm?

"God help the sailors on a night like this!" I said as the rain lashed at the back windows and swirled under the door. The children looked at me as though I were talking seriously and they were wondering about the poor sailors, when the door-latch began to rattle, and in walked an upright object in gleaming black oilskins. It pressed and bolted the door against the driving wind and rain. Then it peeled off an oilskin cape, a sou'wester and lastly a pair of gum-boots, and behold! a man in stocking feet walked across the floor, and drawing a chair up to the fire, he sat down. He ran his fingers through his spiky grey hair and sucked in deep breaths of air through his stumps of black teeth as though he'd suffered Hell and all its furies, then looking up at me, said:

"I was a sailor whin I was a young lad but this weather's the dirtiest iver, faith." So the children had no need to wonder any longer; here was one of the sailors God had helped standing before their eyes. "I'd be destroyed but fer the rubbers," he went on, grimacing like a gorilla in pain. Then, with a sudden change of mood, he banged his swinging chair on to its four legs, and peering searchingly into my face, said "D'ye know the cause of the dirty weather, eh?" I must have looked ignorant because he went on, raising his voice as though he were delivering a lecture:

"Geology! D'ye know inything about geology?"

I caught words like 'gulf-stream', 'rainfall', 'strata', 'wind', 'mountains', 'altitude', 'latitude', and the humble 'dirty weather', which lay at the root of all the trouble. He stopped and gazed into my face again, but whatever he saw there gave him no clue to my having taken it in, so he abandoned the subject immediately and shouted:

"Theosophy! D'ye know inything about theosophy?"

He made me feel a very dull pupil, and whatever he said had to be hammered home with all the force he could muster.

"The nuns are nothing without their black robes. 'Tis the robes that frighten the children and make the parents respect them. And the priests are worse! They encourage the people to be ignorant and superstitious."

Then came a jumbled story about the reeds in Cloonee Lake which bent against, instead of with, the wind. It was of course a natural phenomenon he said but the people thought that the lake was sacred and went there to pray.

As he had no intention of wasting his lectures on anyone who wasn't taking them in, he stopped and scrutinized me again. Had he ignited that stubborn timber that was my intelligence? He decided at once that he hadn't—that was all right—he wasn't short of subject matter and maybe if he tried a different line the penny would drop.

"Tell mc, have ye heard tell of an hermaphrodite?"

My astonished expression must have been mistaken for intelligence because he went to town on this new subject! Now he was including the children who were delighted not because they knew what he was talking about but because they recognised some of the familiar, vulgar words. However crude the words, they were still delivered in his impersonal lecturer's voice, which sounded so funny I thought I'd have to think quickly of an excuse to get out of the room before I became hysterical; then for no reason, the subject switched over to China and my hysteria went. But when he was describing how the men and women bath together I was almost off again, and I was only saved by another change of subject. Like a dream wanders from place to place, so we were now in America. Here the story was about a woman who was standing under an apple tree with her lover and she was shot by her husband who was watching her from the porch. Relating this incident made him laugh heartily for the first time but it knocked all the laughter out of me.

He stood up and began to climb into his 'rubbers' again, saying as he did so:

"If ye should want a mess fer the table, I grow ivery kind uf vegetable and I can leave what iver ye want on the strand below, because I pass by there every day in my boat.

"I feel free to talk with the English," he went on, "the people hereabouts are ignorant and I wouldn't waste my time on thim yerra. I am leaving ye a cake of shop bread. 'Tis a change, shure," he said, and placing it on the table he went back into the dirty weather.

It was Sunday afternoon; the children were out playing and I was sitting in 'the room' reading. I had just flung a fresh log on to the red glowing fire when I noticed a slater dart out from under a piece of loose bark, move to the edge of the log and, with antenna waving frantically, peep at the red ashes which lay menacingly below it. I became so interested in the creature's fate that I knelt on the floor and watched it and using a ruler as a bridge to safety, I urged it on, "Come on, don't waste time by looking over the edge or you'll get your behind singed, you egit!" It hid in cracks, under pieces of bark and down holes, but it didn't stay longer than a second. I imagined it saying all kinds of things to itself, such as, "With God's help, I'll be all right in here", then saying ,"Be Cripes! I'm destroyed altogether with the fierce heat in it!" It didn't see the ruler and scurried on to the end of the log and looked over the edge; on its return journey it stopped every second to have more peeps then just as it was about to reach the ruler, it over-reached itself which put it off its balance and it toppled into the fire. A tiny puff of smoke disappeared long before it reached the chimney. I was so engrossed in this miniature tragedy that I had neither seen nor heard the two visitors who were standing in the doorway fingering the door-jamb, examining the beams, and gesticulating excitedly. My first thought was—they must think I'm mad. Then I thought—they're mad. One of them, when he saw me looking at him, ripped a pencil and paper out of his pocket, wrote on it and thrust both into my hands. I read:

"How much did you pay for this house?"

"I don't know; it's not mine," I wrote.

"Whose is it?" he wrote.

"Patsy White's," I wrote, as though I were signing away my very life. They gesticulated to each other again and looked annoyed with my replies which they were re-reading. My fate lay in their hands! Then, without so much as a nod, they left.

Well, I thought, it's no use having any preconceived ideas as to what Irish people are like. I must be prepared for anything—nothing, nothing after this will surprise me.

Paddy told me when he came the next day that they were only two "Dummies" from the town, a carpenter and a tailor, taking their Sunday afternoon's walk and probably curious to see who had come to live in Bridie's house.

18 SLEEPING OUT

THE "dirty weather" was over and we were into spring.

I was kneeling on my window-sill, looking down the fields which were covered with blazing gorse and sprinkled with blackthorn blossom like confetti. The stream was leaping over the rocks and the draught from the water was shaking the primroses and ferns on the bank. The sally trees were in new leaf and were fluttering and waving against the background of the blue sky. Beyond, the purple Reeks towered proudly into the clouds to un-known heights. The sea was meridian blue, and big birds were flying with urgency close to the water. Had I ever in my life seen a spring like this one!

I could hear the children singing at the back of the house, so I crossed the room and looked out of the other open window. They were sitting along the roof of the turf-shed like a row of sparrows. They always got the words of every song wrong so I listened to see what they were making of this one.

> *Adieu, adieu, adieu, adieu,*
> *I will no longer stay with you,*
> *I will hang myself on a weeping willow tree,*
> *And may the well go well with thee . . ."*

"Hi, you lot!" I shouted, "What about sleeping out tonight? We could take our beds out now and put them under the hay-shed in the haggard."

"Ou ya! Oh boys, oh boys! Come on!" Stella said, slithering down the roof followed by the others. And for the next hour there was nothing to be heard but the din of us hammering our iron beds asunder and dragging and bumping them down the bare stairs. Just as we finished putting them together again and making up the beds, two tinker girls walked down from the Old Road and came across to us. "God bless ye, Ma'am," one said, scratching her carroty hair with broken black finger-nails and handing me a tin 'sweet-gallon'.

"Would ye have a sup o' colourin'"—milk, so-called because it "colours" the tea.—

"I haven't any milk; we only have one cow—I'm sorry."

"Thin would ye gimme a dust o' flour fer the makin's uf a cake uf brid, and may ye always have th' bist uf hilth, God bless ye, Ma'am?"

"I haven't any flour either."

"Fer God's sake don't be so hard and gimme a grain o' tay thin, Ma'am, and I'll say the rosary fer ye te-night."

Again I refused—I didn't like them so I didn't want to give them anything even if I had it, though as it happened, I had none of the things they kept on asking for.

"Thin bring me a knife," she said furiously.

"I will," I said just as furiously, "and I'll use it too if you don't go."

They spat and turned away immediately, crossing the fields to Sullivan's, and shouting filthy language over their shoulders.

The children were scared stiff and wanted to carry the beds back into the house.

"I'm staying out here, anyway, if you want to go in you can," I said.

"But if they come back when we're in bed?"

"Let them! There are five of us and only two of them."

But when the time came for us to go to bed, we had forgotten completely about the two tinkers.

Timmy found a huge iron cauldron on Bridie's rubbish dump under the fir trees and he made a turf fire in it and we lay in our beds talking and watching the reflection of the flames flashing on the high corrugated iron roof. We fell asleep with the warm spring wind stirring the roots of our hair and wafting with it the tarry tobacco smell of burning turf.

We were awakened the next morning as it dawned, by a thrush sitting on the end of Timmy's bed and whistling so shrilly we had to cover our ears. Then the speckeldy hen started cackling as it walked along the top of the ruined cabin. Mary jumped out of bed and we all watched her scale the wall and walk along the narrow broken parapet.

"Almighty candle-sticks! A nest full to the top of eggs," she called over to us.

We scrambled out of bed to go and look. There were fourteen eggs and we carried them into the house and said we would eat every one for breakfast. It was so dark and uninspiring indoors after the freshness out that we carried them straight out again and made a fire in the corner of the wall in a haggard and the smoke puffed at one and then at the other. Lassie, drooling at the mouth and waving her tail, waited behind us, grabbing at the bits of egg we were continually throwing to her.

We sat around like a lot of tinkers with the hawthorn tree over our heads and patches of blue sky showing through the scented may-laden branches.

19 FAIR DAY

If we hadn't been sleeping out, I should never have heard Fian being taken home; I knew that she was to be taken back in the spring, but not in the middle of the night. It was bright moonlight and must have been about two o'clock when the man led her away up the fields. "Good-bye, Fian," I felt a tear roll down my cheek and drop on my hand. She was a bad cow in every way, but I liked her because she was so wild-looking and behaved unpredictably. I fell asleep determined to buy her if the man would sell her, although I knew the neighbours would object.

As soon as Paddy came the next morning I told him my plan.

"Arou mad altogether? Te think of that cow atin' all the good grass, and giving no milk in return. 'Twas time enough he came for her, faith." When he saw how glum I looked he said,

" 'Tis fair day today; what about cycling in now to take a look around 'Tis a bit late, but what harm."

The twelve o'clock Angelus was ringing as Paddy and I lifted our bicycles on top of the wall of the Protestant churchyard, out of the way of the traffic; as we walked down into the town we passed a number of people who were already leaving. The air was full of the smell of sweet-peas, cows and thick brown twist tobacco.

"Inything left?" Paddy shouted across to a group of men standing beside their cattle.

"Yerra, not much; ye're too late." they replied, expectorating long streams of tobacco-stained spittle. "I hear tell that Sean-the-harness-maker didn't sell. 'Tis a fine animal he have too, but he didn't git the price he was askin', so he took her inside agin."

"Come on, Harry, we'll take a look round first," Paddy said, turning and walking along Shelbourne Street into Main Street, where a man was standing beside a group of beautiful miniature black and white cows.

"Hello now," Paddy said to him. "The missus here is lookin' fera cow. D'ye know if there's inything worth having around?"

I was introduced to Tommy-the-Master, and he shook hands and said, "Welcome to Ireland. Now, Ma'am, what do you think of my Dexters? Perhaps we could make a deal?"

"Bridie's land's too cross fer Dexters," Paddy said, "their paps would git destroyed with the briars, but they're nice little animals, all the same."

I would have loved to have had one of them, but apart from their size, they were too dear.

At the bottom of Main Street a crowd of people were standing over a huge cart-horse that was lying on the ground.

"She'll niver agin' git up, yerra," said an old man between ferocious puffs at the stump of his clay pipe.

"Arra, she haven't a chance in the world, and she gone tin year," another agreed crossly.

Two young tinkers in raggy clothes and wearing gaudy neckties, pushed their way through the crowd, and a foxy-haired one with a mass of freckles put his finger and thumb into the horse's nostrils, while the other one grabbed her tail with both hands. They both tried to heave it up on to its feet, shouting, "Git up outa that!" The horse's legs toiled madly trying to find a grip, and managed to struggle up half-way; then it fell back again and rolled on its back exhausted, its huge pale belly looking more like a bloated sea-animal than a horse.

"Come on, Harry, we'll go and have a cup o' tea at my mother's house," Paddy said impatiently. His mother and sister lived at 'Connor's Corner'—so-called because Miss Connor lived there in a back room with the windows boarded up so that no chink of light could penetrate. She had been deserted on the eve of her marriage and had never been out since. Paddy's sister looked after her. We passed a lot of men 'lousing around' gossiping with their backs against the wall and passed through the hall into the kitchen at the back of the house, where Paddy's sister prepared tea and boiled eggs for us. Did I like Ireland, they asked, and wasn't I the great woman to settle in Killah after having lived in London? It was no use my denying the latter because England meant London only to every-one in Kenmare.

"We must hurry on now," Paddy said, wiping his mouth with the back of his hand and getting up. "Have ye forgotten entirely what we came te town for?"

Out on the street again, we saw a man standing in the gutter, singing—if it could be called singing—some blood-curdling song about the 'bloody Sassenachs'. I was interested and wanted to hear it.

"He haven't a splink, that one; he don't know whether or which. Come on," said Paddy, "ye'll have plinty time te stand about after we has the cow got." There was a nice-looking cow in the square which

Paddy examined all over, opening its mouth and feeling its ribs and back; then he noticed that its two rear udders were joined together.

"I mint te tell ye about that," explained the owner glibly. "I'se not the kind te desave a woman, and I'm tellin ye, she'll have no regrits if she makes a deal wit me. Thim paps are not a bit o' harm in the world. She's a fine animal, God bless her! That ye can see fer yerself, and she gives more milk than many of thim perfect ones, faith!"

"The price ye're asking is too saucy fer a faulty animal," Paddy said, walking away. We went into Sean-the-harness-maker's next and found him at his bench in the shop making a halter, but he stopped work at once and took us into the yard at the back, to show us his Kerry cow which was standing in a white-washed stall, bedded with clean straw.

"I'll never manage such a big cow," I said.

"Big or small, it makes no matter so long as she gives the milk, faith," Sean replied, "and she'll spill the bucket over fer ye morning and avinin'—what's more, ye'll git plinty butter outa her."

"She's a good cow all right," said Paddy, wavering, "but the price is a bit high and she gone tin years."

"I tell ye what I'll do," Sean said, "seeing 'tis a woman I'm dalin' with, I'll give ye back a pound luck money."

" 'Tis a dale thin," Paddy said, shaking him by the hand, and Sean-the-harness-maker clapped his other hand on top of Paddy's to clinch the bargain.

We left the cow there till we were ready to go home, and wandered round the town. We saw Timmy standing beside a man with a roll-penny-board, and of course we had to turn out our pockets for more pennies for him to lose. A young man was playing a violin, made of thick white deal, which he'd made himself.

"Ye have a lucky face, Ma'am. Gimme a shillin', Ma'am, and I'll tell yer future," said a tinker woman, blocking my way.

"They see ye're strange. 'Tis as well I'm with ye," Paddy said, pushing me past her. The 'coalkeys', so-called because they came from the coal quays in Cork, were standing on their built-up stalls, shouting out their wares.

"Five crown fer the smock," said one holding up a knitted jersey and tapping it professionally with the back of his hand. "Three crowns den and dat's fer nathin'. T'would be twice the price if ye wint inta a shop fer it, bedad! And ye're standin' dere wit yer pockets fat out wit money, and ye won't lit it loose, aven when ye can see 'tis a bargain . . . a crown den; I had a right te give it te ye in the first place, instead of wastin' me time wit the bibblishin' and clitter."

I wanted to stay and listen but Paddy said we must get the cow home before Sean locked up the shop.

20 DOURUS SCHOOL

"THE craythur fell away a fright since she was sick," Mrs Sullivan said when she met me the morning I was taking Joey to Dourus School, but she had every chance of getting well because the weather had turned fine, and although the distance to Dourus was the same as to the Convent, the pace was bound to be slower, because she was calling for the Barry children. Three of them were even younger than herself. She always had difficulty in walking in shoes, and as none of the country children wore them, she was delighted to go barefoot.

Every morning she set off with her checked satchel on her back and a coloured apron covering her long dress—all the children wore their clothes three-quarter length—and her scrap of hair tied in two stiff plaits. She chose the muddiest parts to walk through because she liked to feel the mud squelching between her toes and she liked having it washed off when she walked through the stream on the way up to the Old Road. As soon as she and the Barry children were on the road they would play horses, not with bowlies like the others, but they themselves would pretend to be horses, whacking their own behinds with sticks and shouting "Git outa that, guan there!" They'd run, twist, kick their legs up, fall, roll on the grass, and do everything a badly-behaved horse would never do. When they got to Hanny Dinny's house, they'd stop for a rest. She, seeing them sitting on the side of the road,

89

would ask them in for another breakfast, and if by any chance they weren't asked in, they would go into the fields and play 'houses', and eat their lunch sandwiches as part of the game. It didn't matter if they were without at lunch time because they could always run over to Mrs Macarthy's and be given an apronful of apples, or else they could buy a penny packet of biscuits at Dinny Island's pub. They used to play in the same field as the bull but it never took any notice of them. Then on they would go again, down a steep, stony hill and over the Dromuckity river, and as they were passing the chapel, Joey would say—having learnt all about the Catholic religion by going to Mass with Timmy and Mary:

"If the chapel doors are shut, we'll have to say the 'Hail Mary' seven times, and if they're open we'll have to go in and do the 'Stations of the Cross'." This always impressed the Barry children who would look at her with awe and say, "Isn't we very holy, Joey?"

They made a point of not arriving at the school before 'The Missus' because they were frightened of seeing the fairies that occupied the school-room during the night. They said that if you listened at the door you could hear the dancing of little feet and that every morning The Missus had to tidy up the books that they had thrown about during the night. Dourus School was steeped in the mystical. One day, blue sweets were thrown into one of the windows set high up in the wall. The Missus told them not to touch them because they were "Poison sweets" and, when they ran to the door, they saw a man in a long cloak disappearing into the pine wood—a stranger never seen before or since.

They played on the strand, which was just across

the road or the river, which swirled over boulders and rocks and under a bridge to meet the sea or the wood, or on the road, where they played taws—marbles—and on rainy days they played in the chapel. 'Chapel Din', whose farmland bounded the school walls, and who kept the chapel in order, had a lot of children who were too young to go to school and they played in the chapel too. They went in fear and trembling of the scholars who teased them mercilessly. They would hide behind the altar and jump out at them making hideous faces. "Go away, ye dirty bitches, go awa-a-a-ay", they would scream in terror. When the weather was very bad, Chapel Din's donkeys and goats and even his geese would find their way in there, and the children would ride on the donkeys, be chased by the geese, or butted by the goats and, considering all this, the chapel proved to be as good fun as any other place to play in.

When it was sunny their play time was extended indefinitely—until The Missus clapped her hands. Then they'd come back and sit on the wall and have their lessons out of doors in the shade of the pine trees.

Joey used to love listening to the Bible stories which were all new to her. She would come home and repeat them to the others, thinking that they'd never heard them before either, and they pretended they hadn't—just for laughs.

"Adamaneve lived in a garden full of apple-trees, but God said that they hadn't to eat any of the apples," she would begin eagerly.

"Who's God?" one of them would ask.

"He's the king of Ireland, shure," she'd reply proudly.

"And what about Adam; was he allowed to eat the apples?"

"Adamaneve, you egit! That was the woman's name."

"And what was the garden called?" someone else would ask.

"Purgity, or something like that I think it was. The Devil said to take no notice of God and eat the apples," she went on.

"Who was the Devil?"

"He was a worm, shure."

"But how can a worm talk?" they'd say, trying to hide their laughter.

"How do I know? I'm not religions—She didn't know that if she ate the apples she'd be taken to Hell!"

"Where's Hell?"

"Athlone, I think it was."

"You fools!" she'd say scornfully, when they were rolling on the floor with laughter.

Then she'd begin her arithmetic home-work in Gaelic and I would listen with wonder, thinking what a clever girl she was. This is what it sounded like to me:

"Ochdeogga nay screeches a nay agus ballatta hain agus a hain herschuct a nay oner a nay ne fay di lum a nay oner shadiogga shoct agus ballatta hain agus a hain a do oner tree a hain."

"Teach me that, will you?" I asked her.

But I wasn't able to pronounce the simplest thing so she gave it up, saying I was a fool.

She was never home before five, although they came out of school at three. Sometimes she was so late I would go looking for her. On one of these occasions I found her on the road throwing stones over a wall at an old man. I was shocked, and I was shocked to hear him blaspheming and throwing stones back at her. When she saw me she dropped her stones and came running up smiling.

"What was all that about?" I asked.

"Just Tiug Padeen. He waits for me every day to have a fight, shure."

The spirit of Tir-na-nOg was everywhere!—Even in this old man of eighty.

Another time it was after six o'clock and still Joey had not come home and I was just about to go in search of her when she walked in trailing her satchel. The strap of her apron was broken and hanging off her like a crooked picture on a wall. Her ribbons were undone hanging by a few hairs and her face which was smeared with grime, bore a far-away expression. We all burst out laughing at her.

"What are you laughing at, you egits?" she said, glancing up with scorn.

"Where have you been all this time?" I asked.

"Fighting," she said, as though it were quite ordinary.

"Who were you fighting and what for?" I went on.

"Timmy Dan Mick pulled a tuft of hair out of Eila Dan Murt's head and made it bleed."

"Good Heavens!"

"I pegged a stone and hit him on the ear."

"Did you hurt him?"

"I did in my eye! But he said he was going te complain me te the Missus."

"But it's after six o'clock, you can't have been fighting all this time!"

"We went te the spring well for a drink and then we ate sloes."

Sloes and spring water—what a feast for conquering heroes!

Every day she had a tale to tell: drunks on the road, a ferocious stallion being taken to the mare, or a cow going to dairy (the bull). Once the horse carrying the mail car "took head" and with broken leads flying, it never stopped till it reached its stall in Kenmare. Other times she'd come in with both hands gripping a bunch of cowslips or bluebells or else an apronful of mushrooms or black-currants given to her by Mrs Sullivan in exchange for "the news".

Each day brought a new adventure.

21 FREEDOM

MARY and Timmy were still very shy. We couldn't
understand one another and that may have had something to do with it. They tried so hard; looking at me
earnestly and trying to get my intonation and even my
expression as they repeated word for word everything
I said. Stella and Joey on the other hand picked up
the Kerry accent so quickly that in the end I found it
difficult to understand my own children. Then it
seemed to come without our realizing it and we were
able to understand each other and everyone else
around.

I did everything I could think of to break down the
barrier of shyness. It was heavy going, but every
incident helped a small fraction . . . There were no
taboos of any kind and our language had never been
restricted. Quite a new lot of vulgar words and
expressions came our way and we weren't slow to use
them. This gave them confidence to *say* whatever they
liked anyway.

Everyone helped without knowing it, Mrs Sullivan
by having an open door, and a table where they could
help themselves to whatever was going. She was only
too pleased to have them in order to hear the latest
news—any news was eagerly listened to. Then there
was Paddy who teased them *all* the time. One day
Mary put her mouth down to drink out of a pail of
skimmed milk which was standing on the floor for the
hens, and Paddy pushed her head right into it. She

cried while he roared with laughter but even this shock
treatment did some good by making them more alert
to Paddy's tricks and to everything else around them.
I got it into my head that if only they would shout as
hard as they could it would loosen them up much
more, so I made up a game called "Tig-round-the-
house". The house stood in the middle of the fields so
there were no obstructions. The four of them would
run round and round while I chased them, then I
would alter my direction and come upon them at a
corner unawares, which made them scream with shock,
and if they didn't scream loud enough, I would catch
hold of them push them on to the grass and pummel
them until they shouted for mercy.

Stella helped to break down their shyness too, by a
game she called 'concerts' and she made everyone
join in. I was the audience—and Paddy too—if he
happened to be there. She put a chair by the side of
Bridie's flour-chest which became the stage! The
opening chorus was one they had picked up in Kenmare, every verse ending with "all because he went to
bed with his navvy-boots on". This was followed by
individual songs and then a play. Little Red Riding
Hood and Jack and the Bean Stalk I saw in quite a new
light! Timmy and Mary had never heard of them
before but they were given parts and I was an appre-
ciative audience.

Then later when the weather turned hot, they had
still more freedom. They bathed in the sea and,
although Mary and Timmy had never been in the
water before, they soon ventured in after watching
Stella and Joey.

Then one day it was Stella who suggested that they
should all "mouch" from school. They started off by

playing ball on the road, then they went down on to
the strand and played in the sea. Joey and I happened
to go down in the afternoon and we saw them running
to hide from us behind the rocks. I called to them to
come out, and they came, expecting a telling-off, but I
said how sensible they were to stay away from school
on such a lovely sunny day. I was glad to see that they
had the courage enough to do it. Eventually, they
felt they could really do and say anything they
liked, but they soon found out that they were
mistaken.

One day Timmy ran up to Sullivan's and straight
into the kitchen and with a twitchy stick knocked the
lamp off its nail, sending the glass globe splintering
into a thousand pieces on the flagged floor.

"Clear!" shouted Mrs Sullivan, snatching up the
twig-broom to hit him, "and learn to conduct before
ye come back agin."

Mary who was already there drinking tea, got up to
follow him.

"Come ye back and wash yer delph," Mrs Sullivan
shouted to her.

"Wash it yerself," Mary shouted back, "haven't ye
the whole day to do it in, instead of sitting there
snuffing."

"Ye lighting bastards! Clear, the two of yers! Ye're
wild out, and if ye dare te come back I'll give ye a belt
with a 'rubawn'."

They came home in a funny humour. Having left a
lot of rubbish lying about in the kitchen I asked them
to clear it away.

"Poo! Lave it where it is, 'tis no harm, shure," they
said, shrugging—but I insisted.

"Must be ye can do it yerself," Mary said.

"Yes, clear it yerself. What do we care about the trashy old house?" Timmy added.

"Let's go and live in the cow-house" Stella said, siding with them at once.

"We will," they both agreed, racing after her.

I was shocked; shocked at the thought of them sleeping out there and also by their abnormally wild behaviour. But I had to let them do it even so. They went off to the rubbish dump of Bridie's under the fir-trees to see what they could find to furnish their new apartment. I watched them carrying in old kettles and grid-irons and dragging armfuls of ferns for their beds and a sack of potatoes. Smoke began to waft up out of the old chimney, which probably had never been used since the time when it was the farm-house thirty years before. They sent Joey into the house for butter and salt and anything else she could steal without my seeing—of course I saw everything but was only too glad that they were going to eat some decent food which was one thing less to worry about. Joey was thrilled to be acting as their go-between and to be treated as someone of importance—for once.

By night-fall they were as black as miners! They shut their door and thin shafts of candle-light filtered out of the broken windows into the mist. They were laughing and talking and altogether enjoying themselves, and there was no need for me to worry about them—but I did. I thought they might get bitten by rats or catch pneumonia. Lassie and a dog we were keeping of Paddy's, I hoped, would keep the rats away. I went to bed very early and pulled my bed over to the open back window so that I could listen for any emergency. After a while they blew out their candle and all was quiet. I was just beginning to relax a little from my alertness and doze off when pandemonium broke out, screams and yelping dogs sent me leaping out of bed. In my panic, I couldn't find the door-latch, then just as I found it the noise died down and I heard them roaring with laughter. I got back into bed my legs feeling as weak as water and my heart thumping against my ribs. After some time there was silence once more, but sleep was out of the question. I lay blank and listening. After about another hour I heard them scuffling about and whispering under my window, and I could see them in the semi-darkness with their backs bent, creeping about looking for sticks and carrying turf in from the shed, and soon sparks began to pirouette up out of their chimney into the blackness of the night. There was no more sleep that night! They talked and laughed for the few remaining hours. As soon as it was light they emerged and stood under my window calling me. I took my time to put my head out of the window and then I pretended I'd been wakened out of a deep sleep.

"Let us come in, Harry, it's awful in the cow-house; we never slept a wink."

You're telling me, I said to myself—I was quite astonished at their filthiness and degeneration in one day and one night.

"All right," I said, "I'll throw you out some soap and towels and a change of clothing and you can wash in the stream and then you can come in."

I had a blazing fire and the kettle boiling for tea when they came in with red polished faces and smiling from ear to ear. Breakfast was hilarious that morning. The noise in the middle of the night had been Lassie and Paddy's dog, Rose, having a fight on top of them. Then without my saying a thing, they began to plan jobs; everyone had to make his own bed and take turns with the washing-up and sweeping, and everyone had to do their own washing. Timmy volunteered to get the dry sticks to boil the water for the zinc bath, if Stella and Mary would wash his clothes. After breakfast they ran up to Mrs Sullivan's and were allowed in once again. The pendulum had swung exaggeratedly from shyness to wildness and now it was normal, but they were still far from being paragons!

PADDY and I had lots of quarrels which never lasted
very long; sometimes he stayed away for a whole week,
and then suddenly he'd get over it, and we'd see his
beaming face coming over the brow of the hill, and
last week's quarrel would be that day's big joke. He
even went off to England once.

" 'Tis no harum for him to cool on the overan side,"
Mrs Sullivan said, when she heard of it. After a few
weeks' absence we thought we'd lost him for good
and all, but he turned up again. He told us he had been
carrying a hod of bricks up the side of a house and
suddenly he thought of the mountains and his dogs,
and went back down the ladder, dropped his bricks,
and walked off without telling anyone. The day after
his arrival he was back on the farm working as though
he'd never left, except for all the strange stories he had
to tell about England. I wish I'd seen England through
his eyes! I don't suppose any of the stories were true;
he only wanted to make us laugh.

This is how one of our quarrels began. I was blowing
the fire up with the bellows, and the more it poured
yellow smoke without any flame, the crosser I became.
The children were expected back from school any
minute, and their potatoes were still uncooked.

Paddy, who was sharpening and setting a saw, got
up and walked out without saying a word. I heard him
banging away at something but I was too engrossed
and cross to take much notice, but when I heard loud

splitting and a heavy thud, which shook the house I rushed to the back door. There was Paddy, stripped to the waist, his new American axe hanging from his hand, and his foot resting on the fallen trunk of the ash tree—the shapely ash tree which grew by the corner, and took away some of the ugliness of the house.

"God! what have you done?" I managed to say.

"I was sick and tired of hearing ye grumble about the damp turf," he said.

"So out of temper you cut down the tree."

"I did not. I cut it down because ye need firin', and what's an owld ash inyway? Doesn't it take all the nourishmint outa the ground so's nothing can grow near it?"

"And why didn't you go and cut the sally trees on the stream bank when you know they need cutting?"

"Ash is the only wood that'll burn green, and sallys take a year to dry out. Ye ought to know that by now." Then after a long pause he went on, "There's not a person in the country that thinks like ye all over an owld ash plant."

"You deserve to be living in the London slums where there are no trees if you don't appreciate them except for burning them. And I'll fling that axe into the sea when I get hold of it."

To think I'd given him the money to buy it too! It suddenly took on an evil quality with its long, smooth, white shapely handle and its razor-sharp steel head —ugh! The tree-stump, surrounded by saw-dust and wood chips, faced the sky, and the tree lay beside it covered with black sticky buds and bunches of tender new leaf, fanning out in stiff shuttlecock shapes; it lay still, unconscious that its life had ended; in a few hours

the leaves would be limp and dying. The ash tree had
been chopped down to boil a pot of potatoes!

Instead of Paddy walking off home and saying "I'll
niver agin look near ye," as he usually did, he marched
angrily into the kitchen and came out carrying a treacle
tin full of nails, a saw and a hammer. I watched him
with hatred sawing the branches off the fallen tree and
slashing off the leaves. His face was red and he was in
a fury. Then, cutting the wood up into lengths, he
nailed two pieces together and flung it on to the grass
—it was a cross!

He's going off his head, he's going to kill me, and
stick that cross up. But no—he was sawing and nailing again, and another cross was flung down. God—
then himself?—crosses were piling up on the grass—
the children too, God Almighty! He was pale now and
he worked with deadly precision like a machine. I
thought, 'If only he would miss and hit his thumb,' to
break up this mood. Then he picked up the crosses and
began nailing them all together, and in a few minutes
he placed an object upright on the ground and looking
at me, he said:

" 'Tis a horse, ye'll niver cut up the tree without one."

"You can have the tree—you can burn it green; I
won't!" I was off again! He wasn't going to stand
for any more! He grabbed his jacket and went. The
children ran down from the old road and, seeing the
horse leapt on to it, calling it "Lightning" and treated
it so badly that before the week was through, it, like
its name, was there for one brief period, then gone.

23 THE CATS

ONE of Patsy's cousins from Gleninchaquin came to see us, bringing us a cat. We looked into the top of the bag and all we could see were two yellow terrified eyes looking up at us. The next second it leapt out, and streaking across the floor like a weasel, it shot out of the back door and disappeared.

I put a saucer of milk on top of the wall every day and every morning the milk was gone—but anything could have taken it. We didn't see it for weeks after this and we thought it had gone for good, until one day we went down to the strand to cut seaweeds and there it was! We had disturbed it eating a lizard. It dived into the woods leaving only the lizard's tail which squirmed and twisted and stood on end like a miniature snake. The children jumped round it scream-ing until it lay still. Weeks passed before we saw the cat again; the next time was up the mountain. It ran across our path with a baby rabbit hanging limply from its mouth.

One morning, weeks after, I went into the hen-house and something, that felt like electrified silk, brushed against my bare legs. I wheeled round to see the cat jump over the wall into Doyle's. A huge dead rat lay on the floor of the hen-house grinning up at the rafters.

Shortly after this we discovered that it had begun to sleep in the cow-house and we kept glimpsing it more often. I put food as well as milk in there and it accepted it, and, us but we had to keep our distance.

The day when it actually came into the house we all stood back feeling quite honoured that he should want to join us. We treated him with respect and—as he disliked being petted—he stayed, sleeping on one of the beds all day unmolested, until the evening when he went off hunting. Sometimes we saw him miles from home but he refused to recognize us on these occasions, slinking away like a mountain tiger, on business we knew nothing of.

He had grown so huge while he was living outside that we kept calling him 'Bigcat' and although it wasn't a very distinctive name, that's the only one we knew him by.

One day Joey brought home from school a kitten, given to her by one of the children—a nasty, scrawny thing that squawked instead of mewing, so it was named 'Squawker' straight away. We never knew what sex it was. It adored Bigcat on sight, but its love and admiration were not returned; Bigcat despised it!

Every evening when Bigcat went out hunting, Squawker followed, wanting to go too. It would seize Bigcat by the neck and get dragged along to the corner of the house where horrible squawks and yowls would ensue. Bigcat had had enough of that nonsense! Poor Squawker would come running back into the house screeching for sympathy. It would lick its wounds for a while then remembering that Bigcat had gone off somewhere it would run out again and yowl, sitting despondently on top of the wall and watching for Bigcat's return. Very often he never came back that same night, but if he did Squawker would jump round him again and get another telling off. It would be forced to keep its distance, eyeing Bigcat, and the least encouragement—or what it mistook for encouragement —it would bound over to him again.

Bigcat wasn't the only one who despised Squawker —Lassie was another. If Squawker came anywhere near her, she would pick it up, baring her teeth and curling back her lips as though it were something poisonous, and carry it down to the bottom of the field shaking it like she would an old rag. Sometimes it managed to escape into the flags that grew thickly in a swampy patch down there, but it never got far because Lassie would drag it out by one of its legs and shake it again and again. After one of these shakings, it turned wall-eyed and never returned to normal again.

It was in the evenings I hated that kitten most! Instead of eating ordinary food it would wait until I was reading in front of the fire and stalk spiders, wood-lice, flies or any other creepy-crawly that ventured out, and the noise of it crunching them up got me on edge. In the end I rebelled—it would have to live out of doors. Although there were plenty of out-houses where it could sleep, instead the children fixed a big box at the back door and filled it with hay and put a bowl of milk inside for it. That evening when it was shut out it got hysterically angry, racing round and round the house screeching like a banshee. When the door wasn't opened for it, it jumped up on the window sill and ran its needle-like claws down the glass, showing the pale under-side of its emaciated body. I went to bed early, hoping that when the light was out it would settle down in its box.

The next morning I heard the children whisper, "Let's get Squawker into bed", then I heard Stella creep down and quietly open the back-door.

"Holy Mary! Come and look at the kitten," she shouted.

Everyone rushed downstairs, including myself, to see Squawker lying stiffly stretched out on the slab of cement outside the back-door, quite dead, its bony legs coated up to its thighs in wet cow-dung. I shuddered and thought it was my fault. But at the same time I was glad to see the last of that unhappy creature, which could hardly be given the name of cat.

Bigcat still went out hunting every evening. If he stayed out all night we thought nothing of it but when it was longer—two or three days—then we knew that he had been caught in a trap, but he was always released, and came home on three legs, holding up one swollen paw resembling a boxing glove. Then when he didn't turn up for a whole week gloom settled on the household. We searched the fields and woods calling him continuously and looking for likely places where a trap might be set. We were over in Doyle's land when Joey put her foot on a trap and screamed so much I thought she was injured for life. I couldn't open it in my panic and had to send Timmy to fetch Mick Sullivan who soon released her. The teeth had clamped on to the hard skin underneath her foot and luckily she wasn't hurt at all.

Ten days passed without any sign of Bigcat. Then in the hot afternoon sun I saw him at the bottom of the field limping up towards the house. I ran down to him and was horrified to see the condition he was in. His front paw was hanging by the tendons and the matted fur had left the bone and all around it was suppurating flesh. He was skin and bones and wet throughout with sea water. Whoever had freed him from the trap must have thrown him into the sea!

He looked up at me with his beautiful, yellow eyes that said, "I trust you, I'm lost, help me." I let out a great sob and carried him into the house. I put him in a box of hay and warmed up some milk for him but he wouldn't look at it. I tried a beaten egg and milk but he really wasn't able to take anything. His eyes said, "I'm sorry I'm causing you this trouble but I'm scared and ill." I bathed his paw in warm water and disinfectant and wrapped it up with healing ointment. The next day he limped out to the hay-shed and lay down in the long grass that grew round one of the posts.

What could I do? If I sent for the vet, he would cut his paw off and that would be worse than death for such a wild creature as Bigcat. Maybe there was a chance of its healing. I kept going out to see how he was, then in the late afternoon, when the children were back from school, he had left his nest. I searched everywhere and eventually went into the hen-house. And there I found him curled up and dead with angry blue-bottles buzzing about him.

"Have ye seen a ghost?" Mary said when she saw me coming out of the hen-house.

"Tell Stella to put Bigcat in a box—he's dead in there and I can't do it and I'll go and dig a hole up by the stream."

I found a place above one of the waterfalls. The spongy turf there was covered with camomile daisies which filled the air with their musky odour. A boulder was standing beside it and I picked a white stone out of the water and wrote on it "Bigcat"—that was all.

24 A CAKE OF BREAD

I HAD a minute thorn in my finger and the more I poked and squeezed it the further it buried itself in, so I gave it up in the end and went out into the garden and planted a hundred cabbage plants. When I came back into the house my finger was purple and pulsating, so I poulticed it with a lump of hot soggy bread, thinking by the morning it would be drawn up to the surface, but in the morning it was swollen and much worse. Paddy had to milk the cow for me, I wasn't able to do a thing. I went to bed in the afternoon feeling ill and in the evening I asked Paddy to tell the Doctor to come up. He came that same evening but instead of coming straight up to see me he played boomerangs with the children in the field. Eventually he remembered what he'd come for and took the stairs two at a time and came laughing into my room. He examined my finger and got out a box of shining instruments which put the fear of death into me. But he had his own methods for quietening the patient, and making what he had to do painless. He told me he had just been along the road to visit Din R. who had to have a slight operation on his throat; the room was so dark he lit a match to see into his mouth and forgetting that the stuff he was using was inflammable, it burst into flames, and, while Din R. was looking in wonder at the fire shooting up to the beams, he performed the operation. When it was over Din R. said: " 'Tis great out, the fire, Doctor, and there was no pain in it at all, faith."

While I was laughing at this story he took the opportunity to dig away lumps of flesh out of my finger.

I felt slightly better after it had been lanced and the pains which I had had in my arms and back were disappearing and my temperature fell, but the poison was still in my blood—which made me irritable beyond words!

Paddy suggested that I should get up for a while and that it was a good chance for him to show me how to make bread because he said, "the stuff ye make will have us all kilt," so I put my dressing-gown on and went downstairs feeling like a tender, new leaf without body and quite unable to stand up to any rough weather. I sat down on the one-and-only easy-chair, which was mis-named in this case—one of the springs reared up at my back and tried to push me off. Normally I shouldn't have noticed it but I felt that I was up against insurmountable odds, and almost cried with anger.

My bread-making lesson began. He started from scratch—so that in the future, I wouldn't be able to plead ignorance. He brought in an armful of logs and turf, and the bang of them being dropped on the floor was like a stone hitting my temples. Then he knelt on the floor and made the biggest fire the room had ever known, so huge that the chimney caught fire bringing clots of glowing soot down which went whizzing across the polished cement floor. I had to tuck my feet under me to keep out of the battery of soot. My eye-lids and upper lip began to sweat; I was getting more on edge. The next thing was the pot oven; it, and its lid he leant up against the fire to 'warm through'. Then he brought in the ingredients and put them on the table.

He emptied flour into a big bowl and then he crumbled a lump of butter through it with his hands, then came the salt and the baking-soda and after pouring buttermilk into it until it was in the right condition for handling, he turned it out on to the table and the kneading began—I thought he was just never going to stop kneading and sprinkling flour on to it and when I was about to scream "stop it", he stopped to lift the oven away from the fire. He burnt his fingers, so he held one of the legs with his handkerchief and the handle with the tongs. He sliced off a chunk of the butter to grease the oven and it melted before it touched the pan almost, filling the room with the stench of burning fat. " 'Tis a bit hot," he said, slamming in the football of dough, pressing it to the sides with his knuckles and making a cross on it with a knife. Then putting on the lid, he raked the fire out on to the floor and placed the oven on top of the hot 'greasuck' —ashes—and with the tongs, covered the lid with burning turf, announcing that it would be baked in an hour.

No more did the room smell fragrantly of hay and cloves and no more did the flames from the fire dance reflections on the hand-painted mugs that hung from the dresser, nor leap across the red polished cement floor. Only fat-stench and cigarette smoke thickened the air and made our eyes stream tears and the floor was a mess of spilt flour, soot and turf ash.

The poison was raging round in my blood like a serpent lashing its tail and darting its forked tongue; I marvelled at myself being so witty and cutting and wondered was Paddy looking at me with admiration or was it hate? I laughed at my cleverness, but to give him his due he suffered it and made no retorts and the hour passed without my getting a black eye.

The time was drawing near when I would have to eat my own cruel words and his cake of bread, and give credit where credit was due. With his handkerchief and the tongs the oven was now lifted off the fire but when he tried to remove the lid it held fast—he had to get the saw-file to lever it up and when at last it came off it brought half the bread along with it.

" 'Tis burnt a small piece, but that's no harm, shure," he said trying to bang the rest of the bread out on to the table, but it held fast too. After a knife was run round it two or three times, it dropped out, enveloped in a thick crust of charcoal.

"A bit of burn is no harm," he said, sticking all the pieces together to roughly resemble a cake of bread. As no knife could cut it he had to file a piece off for me to taste. He spread it thickly with butter and smiling broadly waited for my reaction.

"Ugh! Soda!" I pronounced, discarding it. He didn't believe me! He quickly broke a piece off and tasted it. "Soda is right! I must have soda-ed it twice," he said sadly.

He didn't wait to hear any more from me and after he'd gone, I went back to bed feeling like the same tender leaf that a child had bruised in its hands.

25 THE DONKEYS

As soon as Paddy turned up one morning, he said:

"Git yer bike and we'll go back into the town. I want ye te see something I've got fer ye—niver mind what, ye'll know soon enough when we gits there." I was apprehensive! It was no doubt something we needed and couldn't possibly do without, but what this time?

When we reached the town, he stopped at his mother's house and led me through the hall into the kitchen where his mother and sister were sitting, but he gave me no time to have a word with them. I had to follow him out of the back door and into the yard, but all I could see there were a few scraggy bantams, and a couple of dreary donkeys, standing under a piece of zinc roofing, sheltering from the hot sun.

Looking around, I said, "Where do we go now?"

"Thim's yours," he said, pointing to the donkeys. "Because of their condition I got thim chape from the tinkers who were passing up through the town this morning."

"How much?"

"Six shillings fer the two; 'twasn't much, shure 'twasn't."

I was too dumbfounded to reply and looked at the two animals with disgust. Bluebottles were burrowing viciously into the deep sores that covered their wasted bodies and tufts of dirty matted hair hung off them from scabs and bare patches. Their hides were twitching, their heads rearing and their hooves stamping to

113

rid themselves of the millions of flies. I flicked my hand over them and they buzzed up angrily only to settle back again in black heaps.

"*You* have them," I said, "—I mean, you have them for your father's farm."

"Haven't they three of thim there already? And ye need donkeys fer bringing your turf down off the mountain and fer the manure, and fer bringing the weeds up from the strand. I can't always git the loan of the ones on the farm." Then, noticing my expression, he went on, "They'll soon pull outa that with a spot o' care. We'll call in at the chimist's on the way back and buy a pot of salve to clear thim up."

It appeared they were mine, so there seemed to be no point in my protesting any further.

I bought dozens of rolls of bandages at the chemist's. "Thim's a cod arou," said Paddy, but I paid no attention to him.

He went off as soon as we got them home, and I got to work on them myself. I filled a bucket with hot, soapy water and disinfectant and washed them all over; while I scrubbed them they stood perfectly still, which made me begin to like them. Then I pressed lumps of salve into every sore and wrapped yards upon yards of bandages round them. When I'd finished they looked ridiculous! I roared with laughter at them, and so did everyone else. I went through this same performance every other day, and soon new hair was starting to grow over their healed flesh, and after a week or two they emerged from their cocoons reborn into entirely new donkeys.

They proved to be good-natured animals but rather small for the heavy work. We called them Patta and Mara—Irish for Pet and Mary.

A month after we got them Mara had a foal—it had brown silky hair with pale rings going all the way up its spindly legs, but the most fascinating thing about it was its nose which felt like soft warm pan-velvet.

The three of them wandered the roads and roamed the woods and strands—they were never to be found when they were needed for work. No wall or hedge could keep ours, or anyone else's donkeys at home; sometimes they would be missing for a few days, or even a week, and then we knew that someone had taken them in from the road and was working them.

The Guards came to tell us about their trespassing on the golf course in Kenmare and warned us that we would be fined if they were seen there again. We did nothing; how could we alter their natures?

Every evening they, and all the other donkeys, congregated on the end of the Kenmare Pier. I think donkeys had the best life of all the animals on the farm—not much work, no restrictions—their foals were never taken from them like the calves from the cows, and pals in plenty on the end of the pier.

LASSIE was waving her tail and looking inquiringly
from face to face, knowing that there was something
afoot, but not quite sure whether or not she was
included in the project. I was making bread, boiling
eggs, and packing food and utensils into a basket,
while the children were collecting the things that were
needed for cutting the turf.

As soon as Paddy turned up we all set off for our bog
which was up the mountain at the back of the house.
After passing Doyle's, we began to climb up Willie
Bess's boreen, a stony lane enclosed by straggling
hedges and tumble-down walls. The honey-suckle and
wild roses were in full blossom and the ditches were
crowded with foxgloves, meadow-sweet, knap-weed
and devils-bit-scabious. The fields on the right were
under potatoes, and on the left—so Paddy told us—
was an old burial ground, full of rocks and overgrown
with gorse and bell-heather. The hot, glaring sun shim-
mered like molten glass above the gorse and the smell
of coconut from the yellow bloom hung in the still air.
Lassie was running around in circles and yelping, not
knowing which rabbit to chase first, she uncovered so
many from under the bushes.

Willie Bess was standing outside his house, curious
to see who was coming up. When we reached him he
said, looking at me:

"Honniman down! I thought 'twas two min comin'
up. I didn't know ye in the trouser. Arou makin' off the

bog? I has mine cut and sprod this long while. Ah well, ye has the fine day in yer favour."

"Come on Harry! We can't give the day speechin'," Paddy said, walking on impatiently. Once past Willie Bess's house, we were on the mountain proper, climbing up a narrow sheep track through the heather and rocks crossing and re-crossing the brown-stained peat stream. Every now and then we came across small dew-ponds and I stopped to look into them. Cinnamon-coloured water-plants were perkily sticking up above the surface of the water and bronze water-beetles pivoting between the stalks and leaves. Two lumbering green beetles stirred up particles of brown fluff from between the roots and just over the surface turquoise dragon-flies staccatoed, dipping their tails in the water every second as though to cool them. I had to run to catch up with the others. Bog-cotton filled the swampy patches together with pink cross-leaved bell-heather, and yellow star-like bog-asphodel. The real ling—or heather—was still in bud, only the common magenta bell-heather spread out untidily.

As soon as we reached the bog, Paddy wasted no time, he flung down his jacket and began to 'skin' the bog with a spade, lifting the top sods called 'scraws' to get at the turf. This was a tough job; the heather held firmly to the ground with black roots resembling strands of iron. As soon as a space had been cleared, he cut the turf with a 'slawn'—a special spade—and I was given a two-pronged pike and told to spread the newly-cut pieces out to dry. I took my turn with the cutting as it was so simple to do. The children helped too but they soon got tired and went off up the mountains. Joey stayed with us and modelled little fat brown figures out of the wet turf, giving them white bog-cotton for hair, blue milk-wort flowers for eyes, and red bell-heather for mouths, and in their hands she put tiny posies of yellow asphodel. The effect was striking and primitive.

We could see the children walking along the ridge looking like tiny black silhouettes against the pale blue sky. Then we watched them descending in leaps and bounds—flying downwards from big heights. They said that they had jumped into mossy patches that sank like wet cushions under them. They were very hungry when they got back and so were we. " 'Tis the hungriest job iver," Paddy informed us. We made a fire to boil the kettle, put on a pan full of eggs and we sat on the turf bank with our bare feet dangling in the black oily water eating our meal. The tea tasted like kippers and the eggs like clotted cream.

"I wish we could live up here and never go down again," I said, seeing Kenmare sunk miles away in the hollow and smothered in a heat haze while we were in this thin invigorating rarefied air.

We packed up at six o'clock because we were all so hungry again. As we passed Willy Bess's, he called after us, "Close the gaps after ye, didn't I give the day looking fer my mare after the last one that was up here?" All the way down the boreen we collected dry sticks so that there would be no delay with the meal when we reached home.

The next time we would be up at the bog would be in a few weeks' time when the turf would be dry enough to be 'footed'.

MOST of the hens had stopped laying so we had to share out the few eggs as fairly as possible, but there were always arguments about who should have them, and today we were in the middle of one.

" 'Tis me and Harry's turn fer the iggs teday," Timmy said.

" 'Tis not thin," Mary contradicted.

" 'Tis so," Timmy persisted, "didn't Stella and me have thim ere yisterday?"

"Thin must be 'tis not yer turn agin teday."

"Oh, shut up, you two, we'll spin up for them," Stella cut in.

"We will shot! And ye win," Timmy said indignantly.

"Howld!" Mary shouted, bringing the argument to a sudden end.

We all listened. There was a terrible hullabaloo going on outside and we ran to the door to see what it was all about. Darky, the cow Paddy and I had bought at the fair, seemed to have taken leave of her ten years and enormous bulk and was prancing foolishly around the field, bellowing as though she were mad. Her bellowing started deep down in her throat, ending with a screeching crescendo.

"What's got into her," I thought apprehensively as we ran up the fields and watched her scramble over the wall on to the Old Road bringing the top stones tumbling about her. Once on the road, she set off towards Doyle's, kicking out her legs skittishly and tossing her head like the cow in 'The Cow Jumped Over the Moon', and if she'd been able to laugh she'd have been screeching like a washer-woman.

Jim Doyle came out of his cabin on the roadside, carrying a pitch-fork, followed by his dog 'Bran' which went hysterically leaping and barking at Darky's throat and bit her ankles. Jim Doyle stood in the middle of the road shouting "Git back outa that" and spread out his arms. The cow swerved round, nearly slipping over on the loose stony surface, and started galloping off in the opposite direction scattering us into the ditches.

"She's goin' te dairy," Jim Doyle shouted after us. "Take her west to Murty's bull."

Take her! It was she that was taking us . . . We ran behind the children shouting and laughing and imitating her antics. "Jasus uf Nazareth! What's all the fururum?" Mrs Sullivan said, coming out on to the road with a stick. Then catching on immediately, she shouted:

"Murty, come you out and take Harry's cow west te the bull."

Murty emerged from the dark interior of the house with his mouth so packed with white bread it was falling out the sides of his bulging cheeks. They had some sort of conversation and his mother seemed to understand what he said through the mass of bread. He took the stick from her and went off behind Darky.

I thanked him and was about to go home when Mrs Sullivan said impatiently:

"Yerra, melaire! Is it east yer going without takin' a look at our fine Derby bull?"

So I started to run after Murty telling the children that I wouldn't be long.

"Lave me alone! Don't the craythurs want te see the bull as well as ye," she said crossly.

The craythurs were delighted and waited for no further invitation from me. We met Bina-up-the-mountain on the way to town but she turned round and came along with us. Two of the Barry children were sitting playing on the roadside and they jumped up and came along too.

We all sat along the low wall and watched Murty lead out his black and white Derby bull.

"Bulla, bulla, bulla, bulla," he sing-songed as he brought him up to Darky. The bull made a rush at her, she swerved, and they stood facing one another. Then Darky bared her yellow teeth and stretching her neck up to the sky, she grimaced like a Chinese death mask. It was obvious what she thought of the Murty bull! But no, that wasn't so they always do that; Mrs Sullivan said. The swerving and faces and Murty's sing-song went on for so long the children got bored and started a game on the road while Mrs Sullivan and I sat on the grass-bank talking. After about half-an-hour Murty came on to the road leading Darky.

"Take her back home now," he said to me. "And kape her shut in the cabin till the mornin' and write the date down on a scrapeen uf paper so's ye'll know the date whin she'll be carvin' ."

Darky's escapade was soon forgotten, but a week later she decided to find a bull of her own liking and she went off just before the time she was due to be milked in the evening. I couldn't think what had happened to her, not only was she missing but all the other animals were gone too. The land was deserted. We searched the fields right down to the strand until it was too dark to see so we had to give up. The next morning I got up early and cycled into town and was knocking on Paddy's door at eight o'clock. They were having breakfast and were surprised to see me. While Paddy was washing his bread down with tea he listened to me telling about the missing animals.

"Most likely she's gone back to her old grazing fields at Kilgarvan," Paddy said, putting on his jacket and going out to get his bike from the side of the house.

After cycling a short distance along the Kilgarvan road we thought we saw them in the distance. " 'Tis thim, all right," Paddy said as we came nearer.

The two donkeys and the foal were stretched out asleep in the middle of the road and their only sign of life was from their switching tails beating up the dust. Diamond, a piebald pony we were keeping on our land for Paddy, was dragging the succulent leaves down from the hedge top. Tamine, a Dexter bull Mrs Sullivan had asked us to keep on our land because he had his shoulder out of joint and their land was too 'cross' for him, was standing disconsolately at Darky's tail, while she stood with her head over a gate bellowing continuously.

We rounded them all up and began walking back to the town, Tamine limping along like someone with one leg shorter than the other, and Darky, with not having been milked the evening before, shedding her milk in two thin streams on to the dusty road.

As soon as we reached Paddy's house, he tied her to the iron railings and milked her there and then in the street, his children running in and out with basins and jugs and ending up with cups—she must have given over a gallon. Then we started off for home, wheeling our bikes behind all the animals as we walked them up Main Street. Everyone was shouting at us from their shop-door-ways, "Is it sellin' up ye are?" "Fair day's a Widnesday, ye've mistook the day, yerra!"

One of the Guards came out of the barracks and eyed Tamine suspiciously, wondering no doubt whether his licence had been paid—it hadn't. Tamine's disjointed shoulder didn't prevent him from trying to mount up on Darky, but as she was a very large cow and he the smallest breed of bulls, he was doomed to failure. He repeatedly ended up on his knees or on top of his head; blood from the roots of his horns trickled through the dust covering his face, his knees were bruised and bleeding and his long, straight eye-lashes were so stuck with congealed blood and dust he could hardly see. The onlookers were enjoying every minute of it—roaring with laughter at Tamine's desperate attempts, but I was too anxious to get them home before he had a fatal injury, to see anything funny in his antics.

As soon as we got back, we sank on the grass, exhausted, but we didn't rest for long.

"I've got an idea," Paddy said, jumping up, "come on, Harry! Dexter calves fitch a lot of money and why not Darky have one so."

He led the cow into the manure dump and told me to hold her there until he found the bull. Then he stood Tamine on the flags above, thus making them exactly the same height. Tamine wasn't slow to realize this and made a wild rush at Darky, but just as he did so she side-stepped, sending him head first into the wet manure. Paddy was rapidly losing his temper; he grabbed hold of Tamine and led him to the stream

and shouted at me to bring Darky. Then he stood the
cow in the water and the bull above on the bank.
Tamine couldn't see for manure all over his face and in
his fluster he fell again, writhing at her feet in the
water and was unable to right himself. His legs were
rotating wildly, I shut my eyes and said to myself, "This
is the end of Tamine—what can I say to Mrs Sullivan?"
but I opened them to a miracle. Tamine, washed clean,
jumped up on to the bank and walked off quite normally, his shoulder having slipped back into place, and
within half-an-hour he was back with his rightful
owners leaving me with a growing reputation for the
curer of all ills.

Darky was still un-mated and we couldn't think
where to take her next, but she took this responsibility
off our hands and went off—this time on her own—and
she stayed away for three whole days. She came back
very early one morning with her udders swollen to
bursting point with not having been milked for so
long. No one had seen her going or coming back so all
we could do was to await her calving with interest,
hoping she'd found a bull of some breeding and that
she would give us a heifer calf we could sell for a lot
of money.

28 THE TINKERS

EARLY one morning and in the splashing rain, a tinker woman with a child gripping on to her skirt, appeared at the back door. The rain was dripping off her lank hair and trickling in rivulets down her dirty chest, her open boots stood out from her ankles and caught the drips off her skirt. She certainly looked wet and I felt sorry for her.

"God bless ye, Ma'am," she began with a pretence of humility, "would ye iver have a smock or a bit uf an auld driss fer the childer," and pulling back its long ragged tweed coat, she displayed its naked body. I gave her some of the children's clothes and she rolled them up mechanically into a tight bundle. Her mind, intent on gain, she went on, cringingly "God bliss ye, Ma'am, and may ye always have only the bist uf health, ye wouldn't have a pair o' brogues that would fit the childer?" I explained that any I had would be too big for her.

"What harrum, Ma'am! Haven't I more shildrun than the one alone! Inything ye have, Ma'am, and may the grass niver grow green under yer door!"

I brought out a lot of old wellingtons and dropped them on the step and she knelt and rummaged among them. "Has ye the cumrade o' this one, Ma'am?" she said, holding one up. While I was looking for the other boot she had a good look round the kitchen.

"I wonder would ye gimme a hanful uf thim annans,

125

Ma'am, and I'll say the rosary fer ye tenight?" I refused to give her the onions.

"Thin a few uf dim petatas?" she said, indicating with her head the sack lying just inside the door.

"A few hungery petatas!" she said after I had given her some. "Fer God's sake, will ye gimme a few more, an' don't be so hard, Ma'am!"

There seemed to be no getting rid of her so I just went on refusing every request until she saw at last that I wasn't going to give her any more, and she went off muttering bad temperedly.

No sooner was she gone than a tinker man walked boldly down from the old road—the men never cringe and flatter and they occasionally smile, which the women never do.

"Good-day te ye, Ma'am!" he said insolently, "would ye have any pomies or warmers ye wantin' mindin'?"

I showed him a kettle that was leaking and asked him how much to have it repaired.

"Tree shallin and dat's fer natin'," he said examining it. I suggested two and he said, " 'Tis nat fer the kittle alone, Ma'am, but fer the ware and wallopin' uf me hammers and me journey back and hither has te be taken inta account—'Tis chape at the tree an' I wouldn't be doing it fer liss thin."

I said I would give him half-a-crown and he went off with the kettle and I hoped we'd seen the last of this new batch of tinkers, but the afternoon brought another, a youth about sixteen, in rags and tatters, a gaudy necktie and with a bunch of decrepit umbrellas under his arm. "Good-day te ye, Ma'am," he said smiling. He had very blue eyes, foxy-coloured hair and was covered in huge freckles that ran into one another all over his face and arms.

"Would ye have iny umbrallas dat want mindin'?"

I told him that I had never in my life owned an umbrella.

" 'Tis the better ye are fer it, a hilla! The wet is nat a bit a' harrum."

As we were drinking tea, I offered him a cup.

"I'se just after it, Ma'am, and may God increase ye store, tanks, Ma'am, all the same."

He seemed embarrassed so I didn't ask him any more. The children, feeling friendly towards this one, asked if they could see his "umbrallas" and putting the ones up that would go up, we all had a good laugh at them.

"Dey're ar'rust and need te be scrope" he said, laughing too, and losing his shyness.

"Th'doll abuv tort oi'd discindid from de hivins in one uf dem tings," he went on, indicating Doyle's house with his thumb. "I gat a fierce land all togithir when she slap up the door in me puss and she all a-trimble, the two eyes uf her druv right trou me, faith."

We had no more tinkers calling that day. In the evening we passed their camp at the bottom of the old road. A young tinker was stretched out in an abandoned position with his head resting in a tinker-girl's lap while she was delousing him. An old granny wearing a man's hat, her face scored with deep black encrusted wrinkles, was sitting humped over a fire. Two tiny children with dresses touching their feet ran by our sides saying, "Gi me a pinny, gi me a pinny," and they wouldn't be shaken off even though we told them we hadn't any.

We were wakened in the middle of the night by their ponies and horses stampeding along the old road and sending every dog in the vicinity barking frantically. The next morning they had moved on. When I saw the sordid mess they had left behind I was sorry I'd given them anything at all: a burst mattress trailed fibre across the heather and ferns, a pair of trousers with a dirty greasy lining caught up on the brambles and a black coat, green with damp and age was lying on the stones. The trampled grass was strewn with dirty rags, empty tins, newspapers, broken pots, charred wood and horse manure.

But what was worse than all this was a horse, about seventeen hands, which they had left behind to die. Its knife-like ribs were almost cutting through its mangy hide and its eyes, were sunken into its wrinkled face which stared unseeingly to the distance. It walked unceasingly along the road turning at the top of the Bell Height and walking back again to the camp on the roadside. For three days it never stopped walking— even in the night it was still seen doing the same journey over again until one morning it was found dead on the road and the Guards had to be sent for to have it taken away; they didn't take it far, only dragging it down to the sea below and leaving it there to rot. It was all right when the tide was in, but when it went out, the smell would "knock ye" Paddy said.

29 THE CAMP

WE became dissatisfied with the hay-shed for sleeping out; it was too near the house and the manure heap, the high roof gave no protection from the driving rain, and anyway we wanted to have the sky overhead and not corrugated iron. So we asked Paddy to build a platform, big enough to hold all five mattresses, on a triangle of grass on the edge of the stream where nothing but fields, mountains and sea could be seen. The children named it 'The Camp' straight away. Lassie and the pet lamb—one which Paddy had stolen off the mountain for us, and a new cat called Sybil, slept underneath; we turned them all out the first wet night, but soon let them have it back again as the rain trickled and dripped on to us from hundreds of tiny unseen cracks. After this, when it rained, we ran into the house, carrying our rolled up beds on our backs, and nearly breaking our ankles on the stony path which was the bed of the stream in the winter. But it hardly ever rained that summer, the water had shrunk to a trickle and people came to it from the surrounding farms as it was one of the few streams that had not dried up completely during the drought.

Every evening we had a bathe and got into our pyjamas and came straight up the fields to bed—but not to sleep—we talked and laughed for hours and sometimes made up rhymes about the things that had happened during the day. Then, as it neared eleven, one by one the children would drop off to sleep, leav-

ing me, with a cart-lamp stuck in a knot-hole in the
wood, to read until sometimes two or three in the
morning—we needed much less sleep when we were
outside. Sometimes I'd just lie and look up at the blue-
black sky peppered with stars and watch them shooting to earth all round me. When the moon was full,
I'd go into another world—the vast continent of the
clear sky where the clouds looked like the snowy
antarctic, and the moon raced in and out of them,
lighting up the earth darkly—like looking through old
mirror-glass. The trees were more intimate with the
night than we were, their presence could be felt as they
swayed in the wind, or even if they stood very still;
they came to life while we slept.

Sometimes I'd lie smelling all the scents the night
air brought out, the honeysuckle and wild roses on the
walls, the freshly cut hay over in Sullivan's meadows
and the mint and angelica which grew in the water
nearby. At the same time I'd listen to all the night
sounds, the leaves clacking if there was a breeze, the
snipe high up in the sky thrumming like plaintive
nanny-goats and the corncrakes in the long grass calling monotonously all night like wound-up clocks.
When it was very warm, bats would flit to and fro
above our faces, making tiny squeaking noises, and
feast on the myriad of midges and gnats. Lassie chased
the water-rats that squealed and scuttled about on the
river bank, whining with frustration because she had
no hope of catching them. The trout leapt out of the
water and plopped back as though they were feeling
the heat too.

Darky always paid us a visit; she'd put her fore-feet
on the platform and stretch up to eat the tender ash-
leaves she was so fond of. I would hold my breath

until she got down in case she slipped and smothered
one of us. When she was around, her hot cow's breath
dominated all other smells. One evening I woke up
after being asleep for a few hours and saw a black
figure standing like a statue high up above the stream;
I hardly dared blink an eye-lid, and after about ten
minutes it moved off. The next day, Babe Downing
said she'd been out searching for her cow because she
was afraid it might have been taken to the fair if it
was on the road; she'd taken a short cut through our
land and was interested to see us sleeping out. Another
time I ran along the path to the house to take off the
fire a cake of bread which I had timed to be baked by
midnight, and as I rounded the corner, a man threw
up his hands and cried, "Mother o' God, have mercy!"
He thought I was a ghost, in my white pyjamas. He
had only come to see if I wanted to buy some rhubarb.
The longer I lived in Kerry, the more I came to realise
that time meant nothing in that part of the world. If
someone woke in the night and found himself without
a cigarette, he'd think nothing of walking two or three
miles into Kenmare to knock up one of the shops for
some. And funnily enough, no one seemed to mind it.

We always wakened as the seven o'clock Angelus
was ringing, our top covers wet with dew and stuck
with the petals of gorse and plum-blossom but when
the sun rose over Mangerton mountain, they'd soon
be dry, and the petals would blow off. Then we'd fill
the kettle with stream water and boil it on the shingle
and sit with our feet dangling off the camp, drinking
smoky tea and eating black, smoky toast. The new cat
Sybil would return from hunting, picking her way from
stone to stone over the stream, with a limp bird hanging from her mouth and a red petal tongue showing.

We would imitate the birds calling from the plum-tree "ye'll shure git the pneumonie", and they would be answered by others down by the sea. One morning Mary ran along the path to the house and came face to face with a huge bull. We watched her, petrified, then after a minute the bull stepped aside and walked off with the hedge brushing over its back, and Mary ran on as though nothing had happened.

Before the children had ever slept out in the open they were all scared of fairies, ghosts and noises in the night, but they very soon found that it was even more exciting than the day-time and that there was even less to fear.

BECAUSE we were all at home on Saturday we made this our washing day. As soon as we had finished breakfast we filled the zinc bath with water from the stream and lifted it on to the stones at either side of the fire. As the bath blocked a good deal of the draught, the firing had to be very dry; if it wasn't, the kitchen would fill with smoke, and our eyes stream tears, except for the one wearing the gas-mask—a present from England—and whoever wore the mask would work away, looking for all the world like a washing machine. It was Timmy's job to find dry wood, and plenty of it, as the big bath full of water had to boil. So off he would go with an empty sack over his shoulders, a saw hanging from his hand, and instructions from us to 'hurry on'. Sometimes he'd come back, after having been away for hours, with a far-away expression, and a few damp twigs in the bottom of the sack.

"Do you think we are going to do your washing for you if you won't do *your* job?" Stella would say crossly, and Mary would add:

"I could carry thim many under my axter." And in the end, he'd have to go off again, red in the face and looking as though he'd like to kill us all.

As soon as the water was hot we would put our dirty clothes into the bath and with a stick, press them bubbling to the bottom. When it boiled we'd get the stick again and lift steaming wads of clothes into our waiting buckets. They always dripped over the edges of the bath and the buckets, making the floor a swilling mess of soapy water, but as everyone was barefoot it didn't matter. We proved the Irish proverb "Dirty water washes clean" to be right, because the floor always looked spotlessly clean after washing days.

Then lifting our buckets up on to chairs we would begin the washing—this was always hectic! We sang all the rowdy songs we could think of at the top of our voices and laughed more than at any other time. When we had finished one bucketful, we would totter to the stream with bent backs and wobbly legs and tip the dead weight of clothes into the deep pool above the waterfall. It was Joey's job to stand in the stream and jump the soap out of them and also to see that none escaped over the top of the waterfall—but they always did. They would lie in sullen lumps and soon as her back was turned they would come to life, elongating themselves and sliding gracefully over the top like liquefied cloth. In the deep thunderous pool at the bottom they would prance excitedly and leap gaily about until a swift current swept them onwards.

We would stop our work and give chase, leaping along the stream-bank through deep ferns, twisting our ankles on hidden stones and dragging ourselves free from the clutching brambles. We would catch glimpses of the escaped garment squeezing itself through niches in the rocks then swirling onwards. Or they would be resting for a while in a side-eddy and we would lie on our stomachs and drag them out on to the bank. Sometimes they would get caught up on an overhanging branch and be swinging, tipping the water, and again we would grab at them, but more often than not, they would waltz round in circles in the swiftly flowing water as if they were saying 'catch

me if you can', and then, with a flick of their tails
they'd be off, peeping and hiding behind rocks to see
if the chase was still on. When they made the sea, we
had to abandon them, and weeks later we'd find a
sock or a vest washed up by the tide and covered
with shells and sea-creatures and no life left in them
any more. But it was worth losing a few things for
the 'gas of it'.

Back to the deep pool we'd go, where the well-be-
haved clothes were lying, waiting for us to lift them
on to the bank, wring them out, and hang them on the
line. We could never go to the bother of wringing
them out thoroughly, so once again we would totter to
where the wire line was tied to two ash trees at either
side of the field, and hang them up, with the water
running out of them and down our upstretched arms.
The clothes were so heavy that the wire buried itself
deeply into the bark of the trees and disappeared, and
the weight invariably broke the line. As we just couldn't
unpeg everything, Timmy stood at the break and
quickly tied the ends together as we pulled them taut.
The wind, rain and sun did the rest, rattling them like
gun-fire, soaking them through and finally bleaching
them snow-white. Mary said:

"If we just hung up our dirty clothes, shure wouldn't
the rain and the wind do the washing *for* us?"

PASTED up on tree trunks and in shop windows were notices for the circus which was to arrive on the coming Saturday. Dozens of circuses came to Kenmare but this one sounded by far the best. The Big Top had five poles and the animal and human performers excelled in their stupendous and unbelievable feats according to the notices; consequently everyone was keyed up for the day.

As Joey walked so slowly we set off in good time and as it was very hot and sunny it was slow going anyway—when we arrived in Kenmare we found that we weren't so early after all. We joined up with the crowds walking up the dusty lane to the fields behind the railway station called "The back o' the Main". This was when Timmy began to get worked up. They had all been irritable with pent-up excitement but Timmy was the worst. Because of the crowds he thought we wouldn't get in. Then he got it into his head that I hadn't enough money for all of us and that maybe he would be the one to be left out. He was almost crying with anxiety until we were actually inside the gate, then he eased up a little, but not much; he had no eyes for anything but the entrance to the Big Top and he was frowning at me for gazing around.

A caravan was standing just inside the gate and an old leathery-skinned hook-nosed hag was leaning out of the half door expectorating long streams of tobacco-stained spit on to the grass contemptuously ignoring the crowds. A canary was silently hopping about in a gilt cage which hung over her head and from the dark interior glinted polished brass and engraved mirror-glass. The circus ponies were grazing under the shade of a group of huge Spanish oak trees that grew on a hill in the middle of the field.

We moved slowly with the others in the queue to the entrance to the Big Top and I watched the bold brassy girl who was giving out the tickets saying, "a shallin'", and greedily taking the money without looking up; she might have been letting in a crowd of chimpanzees for all she knew or cared. We took our turn and were let in, and that was all that mattered to the children—they hadn't noticed any of these things, but now they became all eyes.

We sat on a low seat next to the ring and watched the band come in and take their seats. A lout in rags and gaudy neckerchief played the violin and a sly middle-aged man in checks who resembled a horse-dealer, plucked at a banjo, then the same girl who took our money came in, eating a huge green cooking-apple and sat herself down by the drums and banged away with her free hand without giving a thought to what she was doing except to munch at her apple. The same contemptuous attitude was in every member of that circus.

Ponies galloped in and ran monotonously round and round the ring with a teenager in a dirty pink satin dress sprinkled with sparkling diamanté, straddled across two of their backs; she twisted on her bottom this way and that and did the usual stunts. The clown got in her way, purposely of course, and tried his best to be funny—no one laughed, not even the children. They trotted off and a lot of dogs came into the ring wagging their tails. They were made to jump through hoops and walk on their hind legs. The clown in the meantime had got himself a bucket of water which he poured on the dogs and down the front of his baggy trousers. A feeling of uneasiness was in the air, the lads standing at the back were talking and laughing among themselves; they were up to something but no one knew what until a grass sod came flying over everyone's heads and landed at the feet of the clown, this was followed by another, then another; as fast as they could kick up the grass came the sods until the manager rushed out into the ring and holding up his hands for silence, he said:

"Ladies and gintlemin includin' the boys at the back and the children, I want ye te know that this is no foreign show. We are as Irish as the boys at the back there and we've come straight from the finest place on earth—Dublin city."

"That's dog rough," one of the boys shouted and everyone laughed.

"We've been travellin' fer many days te bring this show te ye here in Kenmare."

"Has ye been over?" (England) another shouted.

"So I'm askin' ye te give the performers a chanct and if the lads at the back will stop peggin' the scraws, we'll git on wit the show."

Just then a sod hit him full in the chest and everyone roared with laughter, and that finished the circus. Everyone began to file out, some laughing and others very angry. The manager made one more desperate attempt to stay the flow but it was no use. The next day the field was deserted. They had moved on to the next small town no doubt to take their money as they did ours and give nothing but contempt in return.

As our land hadn't been ploughed for many years, we couldn't expect to grow a good crop of grass, Paddy informed us, but he blocked a field off all the same because hay was too dear to buy. It proved, as he said it would, to be short, weak grass, and cattle breaking in reduced the amount still more, but it was a big field and we might just about get through the winter on what it would yield.

It was the end of July and everyone else but us had their hay cut and stacked into the hay-sheds and as our grass was beginning to shed its seeds, Paddy thought it was time to cut it before all the good went out of it. The weather was also in our favour, there had been a drought for some months and ours was about the only stream that hadn't dried up. So Paddy said he'd be up the next day to mow it. We had bought a scythe some time ago and now—the evening before— he was setting it to his liking so that there would be no delay in the morning. It was as tricky as choosing a golf club—the grip and swing had to feel just right.

He came before sun-up and the children were all in bed asleep but I had been warned to have everything ready. After a quick cup of tea we set off to the 'lacker' —high field—which adjoined the old road. Our feet were soon drenched by the heavy dew and the birds were swooping about excitedly. As it was the highest field on the farm, we were able to see vast distances; the sea and sky looked new born, puffy coral-tinted

clouds lay light as air in the weak sky and the water
shone like opals. The air was fresh and uncontaminated
and smelt of delicate wild roses. It was horrifying to
think of people in bed heavily asleep.

We climbed the wall over in the far lower corner of
the field and Paddy flung his jacket on the wall and
began the mowing immediately, swinging the scythe
round his back rhythmically as he went step by step up
the field. I followed him with a pike, shaking out the
'swats' and hearing the gritty, swishing sound of the
scythe as it cut the grass stalks close to the ground.
Every now and again he would stop and clean the
blade with a 'sop' of grass then sharpen it with the
'side-stone'—a board covered in sharpening stone
which he kept in his belt—finishing it off to razor
sharpness with the 'side-board'—a board covered in
emery.

Hours later the children came running up to the
field and were sent straight back to the house to fetch
a sweet-gallonful of butter-milk, because mowing was
the "thirstiest job iver", cutting turf being the hungriest. The sun came up over Mangerton and it was hot
but by midday it was stifling. It was a relief when we
came to the 'sleeve' the boggy part of the field where
the grass grew tough and was a milky-blue. The humid
air above the wet part was filled with the smell of
herbs that grew with the coarse grass. It felt cool to be
ankle deep in water but Paddy didn't like it at all
because it was poor fodder and a waste of time cutting
it, but as we were short of hay it would mix in with the
"kind" he said, even the tall flowers that topped the
walls, such as valerian, mullian and angelica were cut
to mix in with the kind too. The scythe often disturbed
wild bees' nests which were buried in the grass roots

and if Paddy didn't run for it, they would sting him on the face and arms. Sometimes he'd have to run the whole length of the field before he'd loose off the angry bees one by one, then when he came back we would sit round and eat the nobbly lump of honey they had deserted—it had a wild, nutty flavour.

It took three days working from dawn to sunset to mow the field and after it was finished Paddy went home for a rest because it also was the most tiring job on the farm. He left us with instructions as to how to save the hay. Each day we had to shake it out and every evening make it up again, beginning by making small cocks and making them bigger as it got drier, until it would be finally made up into stacks ready to be carted into the shed. After ten days of sunny weather Paddy said he would come the next day to cart it in for us, and for the last time we shook it out but as the nights were so hot and dry we didn't bother to make it up that evening—we'd never left it spread out before but we'd have time enough to rake it together when Paddy came and it would have a little more time to have an airing.

That same evening when Jim Doyle was watering his cows at the stream that ran over the road into our land, he shouted down to us:

" 'Tis dangerous wither te lave the hay sprod out and my advice te ye is te git it made up as securely as possible."

We looked all round us at the cloudless sky and said: "He's off his head."

That night we went to bed after a bathe in the sea, feeling cool for the first time, but our cool feeling didn't last for long; the air was still and hot and we began to sweat, and the midges got under our covers until we

were driven almost frantic with bites. Bats flitted
swiftly back and forth feasting on the midges which
had filled their bellies with our blood. The bats must
have had a blood-meal that night! At last we fell asleep
sticky, bitten all over and exhausted.

After a few hours' sleep I was suddenly wakened by
two or three big drops of rain splashing on to my face.
I quickly looked up at the sky and saw a black cloud
right overhead but as it was the only one, and as it
passed over, leaving the starry sky clear, I fell asleep
again immediately. Then after another few hours we
were all wakened by a deluge. We rolled up our mattresses and ran for the house. Joey refused to budge;
she covered her head and went on sleeping. I had to
lift her down on to the gravel and she ran screaming
with annoyance along the path to the house. As soon
as she was resettled into bed, I said, "Now for the hay."

As it was still very hot we went out in our pyjamas.
It was very dark and still pouring rain so we had to
feel our way up to the field. We carried rakes and pikes
and climbed the wall and jumped on to the sharp
stubble in our bare feet. I began to rake at random but
it was no use—we had to throw the rakes away and
get down on to our knees and feel for the hay, gather-
ing it up in armfuls and making it into rough heaps.
Our pyjamas got so wet they gripped on to our limbs
like restricting bands so we tore them off and worked
naked. It was still unbearably hot even though it was
pelting rain. Hay seeds stuck to our sweating bodies
and made us mad with itch.

At last we reckoned we had covered the whole field
so we went back to the house feeling exhausted. I lit a
candle and saw that it was half past four; we had been
working for two hours. Then we caught sight of Stella

and began to laugh; her red, curly hair had gone straight and black and was dripping on to her shoulders; she looked pinched and long faced. We were all scratched and bleeding and our hair massed with hayseeds. We laughed so much we wakened Joey but the more she shouted at us to stop the more we laughed.

At last we calmed down and made a cup of tea and went to bed, lying just where we had flung down our mattresses after the rain. The next morning I went up to the field to see what sort of a job we had made of it and found that we had only missed out a small corner. The stacks were very roughly made but, on the first sunny day we would have them spread out and dry again; however, there were no sunny days for a fortnight and by that time the hay had turned black. We did the best we could with it and Paddy came up and stacked it into the shed. It was heart-breaking after all the hard work and time we'd spent on it. It was a bitter lesson and we would never allow it to happen again. What's more, when the winter gales came lumps of hay were blown out of the shed into the open; and that year we had to buy hay after all.

WE almost lived on the strand all through the summer;
what little work there was in the house was soon done,
and the crops didn't need much attention. It was just
as well the sea was only at the bottom of our fields as
we carried so much down with us. Timmy brought a
hanging pan full of potatoes, Mary and Stella ran into
the vegetable garden on the way and pulled up carrots,
onions and bunches of herbs, while I brought down a
sweet-gallon of butter-milk, butter and eggs. Joey
carried nothing, because on these occasions the pet
lamb always made a bee-line for her and butted her
over, making her scream with annoyance and everyone else scream with laughter. The animals always
came with us; Lassie ran ahead, waving her tail, drooling at the mouth, and barking for us to 'hurry on'.
Sybil, the cat, came behind, weaving through the long
grasses and mewing plaintively. Even the cow joined
us for part of the way, thinking we were off to cut down
an ivy-covered tree for her—sometimes she ate so many
ivy-leaves that it flavoured her milk to such an extent
that it became undrinkable.

As soon as we reached the strand, we stripped off
and went into the sea. Stella, Mary and Timmy picked
up the dog, the cat and the pet lamb, carried them out
as far as possible, then put them down in the water
and had bets as to which would reach the strand first.
Lassie always won. She would shake herself frantically,
then run away and hide behind a rock and peep out to

make sure that she wasn't going to be taken in again. The cat slunk into the woods like a drowned rat, and we never saw her again. The pet lamb jumped into the air sideways, like a wound-up toy whose works have gone wrong. Although they all hated it, we did this every time, not simply for our own amusement, but to clean and freshen them up. After this we played in the sea, sometimes for over an hour, it was so warm. Mary and Timmy soon learned to swim, but she was the more adventurous of the two. She would go far out and dive into the waves, emerging like a seal with her black hair plastered against her face. Timmy swam with short, quick strokes and Stella like a fairy, never allowing a hair of her head to get wet. Joey dog-paddled on the edge, shouting all the time, "Look at me, look at me swimming!" Sometimes Stella, Mary and Timmy would swim along the coast or play on a raft they had made. When we came out we'd all collect dry wood and build a fire between two rocks while someone washed the potatoes and filled the pan up with sea-water. We hung the pan on an iron bar between the rocks. Those potatoes tasted better than at any other time; we ate them in our hands, with a lump of butter and salt on each bite, and an onion or carrot in the other hand. If we had eggs, Timmy would carve spoons out of drift-wood to eat them with.

Sometimes we had to cut seaweed for manure. This was a fine job, because we all worked in the sun without clothes and cooled off in the sea. I did the cutting, holding up the long tresses of weed on my arm and cutting it close to the rocks with the sharp bread-knife. The children carried it streaming over their backs on two-pronged pikes and piled it in a heap on the bank to await Paddy and his 'jennet' and car to take it up to

the field. The weed stuck to our skins and by the time
we had finished we all resembled Africans, and had to
stand in the sea until the weed was soft enough to
rub off.

We always had the strand to ourselves, but once we
saw three naked men running in and out of the woods
like cave men. When they saw us, they ran behind the
rocks, and when they came out with their clothes on
we saw that they were priests—jolly priests who came
over to talk to us and set swimming competitions for
the children, giving the winners pennies.

It was evening before we walked up the fields to the
house feeling as clean and scoured as the sea-shells.

STICKS had been waiting for over an hour to see the children when they came back from school—they were very late. Then Mary burst in, out of breath and wide-eyed with excitement.

"What delayed ye at all?" he asked, "was it that ye were listenin' to the latest news about Lord Craigarven —God rest his soul!"

"The crusher wint west the road," said Mary, ignoring his question.

"Do ye hear me?—Lord Craigarven's dead, did ye not know?"

"'Tis stopped on the line below, next to Steve Dennahey's place," she went on. Stella and Timmy ran in in the same excited state.

"The crusher's below on the road," Timmy said.

"Shure, ye're as bad as Mary, and no news from the town at all about Lord Craigarven," Sticks laughed.

"We're going to get up early in the morning to see it start up," Stella put in. Sticks was entirely ignored; he was nothing but an annoyance, muttering silly things in the background. The crusher was all that mattered. For months previously everyone with land adjoining the line had been preparing for the arrival of the county council to repair the road. They had been clearing the land of rocks and stones, dragging them down on wooden sledges and heaping them up on the side of the road to sell to them. Not only did the stones bring in good money, but the men were employed as

147

well, fresh batches being taken on according to the
ownership of the land on either side. All farm work
was suspended in favour of this more lucrative
employment.

The next morning the children were down on the
line to see the crusher start up at half-past eight, and
I went later to see if they were all right, as they had
been away for so long. But they hardly noticed me;
they were in another world, the fairy-tale world of
grotesque monsters. The men from the nearby farms
who we knew so well were transformed into grey
robots, coated with stone-dust, even to their lips
and eye-lashes; they neither spoke nor smiled, but
only worked like mechanical slaves moving round the
crusher to supply its every need. They dropped rocks
into its gaping iron jaws and it ground them up noisily
and ejected them in heaps of sharp gravel chips on to
the road for the men to shovel into their wheel-barrows
and take away. More robots fed coals into a fiery
aperture in its body, while others slaked its insatiable
thirst with buckets of water which were poured into
another yawning cavity. The whole world seemed to
be filled with its din, and the air all around was black
with the smoke it belched from out of a long pipe
protruding from its iron body.

The steward, resembling a plaster cast, was there to
see that the crusher wanted for nothing. The only
one of flesh and blood and the only one not under the
spell of the crusher was the water-man. He was
employed, together with his donkey and car, to fetch
water from the stream in a couple of tar barrels. He
took his time standing with a foot up on the ditch
bank and chatting to anyone going to or from town,
and when the work was held up for want of water, the

steward, raising his hands to the heavens, would rave, "Where in Christ's name has the bloody water-man got to? Lard God give me patience before I kill him dead wit a shuvell, 'tis cruel, 'tis cruel altogether!"

The water-man came strolling along with a flower between his teeth, unaware of the delay he was causing and of his threatened death. He went off with an injured look after being given the sack in a few controlled words from the steward.

Tomorrow there would be a new water-man and all would be well, but tomorrow spelt disaster!

The children went down early as usual, but the only sounds were of the birds calling and the rattling of horse-cars going along to the town—the crusher stood silently on the grass on the side of the road. Suddenly, they heard a whistle, and another whistle—looking all round them they could see nothing—then a hand coming from behind the wall of stones was beckoning them to come quickly and, to their utter amazement, all our neighbours who had been working for the crusher were there sitting on their haunches with a pile of small stones piled up by the side of each one of them. They told the children to "clear" because there was going to be "murder on". Not wanting to miss this revolt, they hid behind a boulder and shortly they saw in the distance the workmen from Kenmare cycling towards the crusher, and the concealed men, fingering their pile of stones. They watched the workmen lift their bikes into the ditch and fling their lunch satchels down on the grass and walk towards the crusher and they heard a voice shout, "Let her go boys!" This was followed by a volley of stones that flew over the top of the wall hitting the workmen and driving them running back into the ditch for protection. They soon caught on to what was happening and a fierce fight ensued on the road. A small boy cycling towards Kenmare jumped off his bike and gaped with astonishment, then one of the workmen gripped him by the arm and said to him, "Go ye bhoy and fitch the Guards before we're all kilt dead on the road." The boy jumped on his bike and went off like the 'hammers of hell' not daring to look back.

In no time four Guards came cycling to the rescue and stopped the fight and a conference was held on the road. The trouble was that the county council had bought everyone's stones all the way along the road as they came to them, but they had left Furzy Lynch's stones unbought so he had collected his neighbours together to stop the crusher from working until they agreed to buy them. What the outcome was the children didn't know, but an isolated wall of stones is still standing there.

But as it happened Furzy came off better than anyone else.

He and another fellow were clearing his land when they came across a huge rock which they had to heave up with a crow-bar it was so heavy. The extraordinary part about this rock was that it was limestone and limestone didn't occur on that side of the sea inlet—it was all at the over side; what's more it was fluted in the form of a gigantic shell. When they had got it up, they found a heap of 'trash' lying under it mixed up with soil and gravel. They were 'peggin' it into the 'dag' when the local doctor came along in his car and stopped to see what they were up to. He got very excited and piled 'the ould trash' into the back of his car and sent it straight off to the Museum in Dublin. The trash was old—bronze battle axes dating back to the fifth century—they are still in the museum.

Furzy Lynch was sent £50. In one week he had it drunk.

"Thim things should be lift alone! I knew they'd bring him no luck in the end," everyone said.

I was digging up a field of potatoes—second earlies—
and as it was very hot I was wearing only a flimsy
cotton frock and had bare feet. A man, whom I had
never seen before, shouted over the wall that he
wanted to see me and I was surprised to hear his
business. He had written to Patsy in England to ask if
he could take the grazing and she had replied, saying
that if I agreed he could go ahead. He came from
Lauragh—twelve miles away—and his job was to buy
and sell cattle at the various fairs and our land would
be convenient for him, being just outside of Kenmare.
As we had twenty-six acres of grass-land and only a
few animals, I couldn't refuse him. Then after it was
all settled he went off looking worried and saying that
he would let me know—which seemed rather funny.
He evidently went straight to Paddy's house and said,
"I hear tell ye work fer the woman back in Bridie's
house at Killah and I was thinkin' uf takin' the grazin'
there but what class of a woman is she at-all-at-all?
because, faith, she have fierce yalla ligs"—I was only
sunburnt—Paddy thought this a great joke and must
have reassured him, because after the next Kenmare
fair, the first batch of cattle were driven into our fields,
he told the man heaps of lies about me—never missing
an opportunity as usual. There were about thirty
bullocks, a lumbering sour-faced common lot! I felt
them to be an intrusion and this was putting it
mildly.

They stayed down in the lower fields until that night. When I was in bed and just dropping off to sleep I heard the ominous thudding of over a hundred hooves approaching the back of the house; they halted under my open window. I looked out but all I could see was something blacker than the night in a mass below. I could hear them breathing and moving about and their rank, musty smell filled my room. Then they started to fight, horns were clashing, they were snorting and pawing the ground, grunting and coughing. I was afraid to shout at them in case I wakened the children; the smell of blood, mud and sweating bullocks nearly made me sick. I fell asleep eventually, thinking that if there was such a place as Hell it was like this.

The next morning I put my head out of the window and to my amazement saw all thirty of them sitting cheek by jowl, chewing the cud. Their eyes were half shut and the expressions on their faces said, "We knew nothing, absolutely nothing." What's more, they seemed undamaged.

I got up in a fury determined to shift them from the back door. I grabbed a stick and yelled at them to "Git outa that". After whacking all round me they reluctantly got up on to their feet and trundled off, wagging their heads up and down as though I were some pest, but no sooner was I back in the house than they were there again, flopped down and chewing their cud. Over and over again I sent them off but they always came back, till in the end I had to leave them sitting round the back door like a lot of ugly pets. When the sun came up they went down the fields and stood in the shade under the arch of the bridge, ankle deep in the water. But we hadn't peace for long; the gad-flies soon discovered this rich breeding ground and the minute one deposited its eggs in the hide of one of them, the whole lot panicked. With their tails crooked in the air, they galloped up the fields pressing through the gaps in the walls and sending the stones tumbling round them, splashing through the stream near the house, polluting our drinking water with the wet dung that streamed down their legs, and crowded into the cow-house, pushing their way in until it was one solid mass of cattle—too tightly packed to fight, thank God!

Late in the afternoon they came out once more and flopped down outside the back door. Swarms of flies buzzed round them, settling into the corners of their eyes and on to any bare patch on their bodies. The air above was filled with water-wagtails, flitting to and fro, gorging themselves on the flies. In the cool of the evening they at last went off to graze and I thought after this first day they would settle down and behave themselves, but they were all strange to one another, having been bought in twos and threes. Just as they were beginning to grow friendly, they were taken away to be sold and another batch were put in, and the fights started all over again and always under my window. They must have liked the confined space so that the battle couldn't get out of hand. They very soon discovered the hay-field and every morning I would waken at daybreak and put my head out of the window and more often than not they would be in it. I would leap out of bed and run up in my pyjamas brandishing a stick and yelling horrible language at them. They'd look up at me with our precious grass hanging out of the sides of their mouths, then turn skittish and gallop off down the fields to the road. I'd pull the poles out of the gap and send them hurtling down more fields to the sea, hoping they would drown themselves like the biblical swine. On one of these occasions a man going to town on his horse-car nearly fell off on to the road as he turned to look at me. No wonder! My pyjamas were wet with dew and sticking to my legs and I was shouting and waving a stick like a raving lunatic.

I complained about them and the next lot, Doni Mickle said, would be permanent heifers. I was relieved—but not for long. When the permanent heifers arrived, we were sleeping out on the camp as the weather was dry and hot. Their appearance was a great deal better than the bullocks and they behaved all right until one morning when I went to make my bed I saw a white heifer standing with its head over our beds. When I got up to it I saw that it was eating the bed-clothes. It had a sheet half-eaten which I tried to pull out of its throat. I might as well have let it finish it as it was chewed into holes and covered in green slime. The top cover was missing so I suppose it had had a meal of that before I arrived on the scene. I called the children, who were on their way to school, to the rescue; they came running back wondering what the trouble could be. They whacked the heifer away and laughed instead of sympathized. Then they set off for school once more but no sooner were they at the bottom of the field than I was shouting at them to come back again. I had walked back into the house with the ruined sheet and what should I see but the white heifer with its behind sticking out of the front door. It had eaten Joey's vest and pants and was starting on her dress. "Lock it in the cow-house," I told them, "and I don't care if it starves, it's not going to be let out again." This was "great sport" to the children.

That same evening Doni Mickle came and I told

him all about the white heifer, and his only reply was, " 'Tis a hungry time of the year, faith." We went together to get it out so that he could take it home. I had left my milking overall on a nail in there and all that was left was a strip of material with a row of buttons.

EVERY day the cows had to be milked, the hens fed and the crops attended to, so we were tied to the farm and were never able to take a holiday—not that we minded—every day was a holiday—but when I met a woman in Kenmare and she suggested that we went off somewhere for the day in her son's car, which he had just bought for hiring out, I thought it a good idea and told her we would go the very next day.

We were already waiting when he called for us at ten o'clock. We didn't know where to go so the driver suggested Glengarriff and said we could either go over Healy's Pass or take the road with rock tunnels.

I would much rather have gone over the pass, but the children had their way. When we got to the tunnels, they made him drive backwards and forwards a dozen times, and would have stayed there all day if I hadn't insisted on going on. The road ran through the rock and heather covered mountains all the way and our next stop was in Glengarriff at the Eccles Hotel which stood on the edge of the sea. Here the driver left us to go and visit relations and suggested we took a boat to Garnish Island.

It was October and the season was over and the boats put away for the winter but we were told that there were a few men out in the bay scallop fishing. The first one to come in was an old man who said he'd take us immediately. As we were being rowed over he told us all the Glengarriff news which was so interesting that we found ourselves scraping up against the high walls of the jetty much too soon. We climbed the white-washed steps on to the island and watched the fisherman push the cobble off from the wall with his oar. "I'll be back fer ye in two hours," he shouted. "Pull the bell," he shouted again from the sea when he saw us standing there unable to go any further. Timmy found a hanging rope with a knot on the end and he tugged it and a bell pealed out, which like magic, opened a door in the wall and a man was standing in the entrance beckoning us in.

He said: "Folly de pat till ye gits te th'Italian villa, den go tru th'door into th'garden and up the pat te th'Greek timple. Return by th'martello tower and kitchen gardens and I'll be waitin' fer ye when ye gits back."

No one had told us there were any of these things on the island—we could hardly believe our ears! We walked along the tree-enclosed path in silence and awe until we came upon a pink-washed villa bathed in the autumn sun. It was acanthus pillared and had a wrought iron fan-light over the graceful entrance. Through a door in a high stone wall we caught sight of a beautiful enclosed garden; it might have been the one Alice saw through the key-hole except that we could walk straight ahead without any fuss. The sun was beating down into it, bees were humming and rock plants were out in full bloom. The sea-crossing had been so cold and the heat in this garden was as hot as on a summer's day. We walked along the stone-flagged path beside a pool patterned in waxy water-lilies with round leaves almost covering its glassy surface. The air was scented with the delicate perfumes of the rock plants, although their flowers were so small

they were in large, bright masses. We reached the door
at the far end and found ourselves on a path that led
uphill through soft, springy turf, studded with tropical
flowering bushes and trees, each with a lead label
bearing an unpronounceable name.

When we had climbed to the top of this hill we saw
the Greek temple perched on a rock-faced crag over-
looking the sea. The water ran violet up to the mainland where the 'Sugar-loaf' mountain towered up
misty purple against the pale sky and range after range
of other mountains stretched as far as the eye could
see. We went into the temple and sat down on the
stone seats which ran all round the open interior.

"I'm piped with the thirst," Timmy said.

"And I'm starved with the hunger," Mary complained.

So I unpacked the lunch basket and as the wheaten
bread was still warm we had to break it off in lumps
and plaster butter on each bite. I looked around at the
slim Ionic columns delicately supporting the canopied
roof and the fairy-tale scenery all around, then at the
children stuffing themselves—there was no idyllic
grace about them! The contrast was so funny I began
to laugh. Then as though the place was infested with
millions of laughing sprites, I was possessed by them
and I couldn't stop laughing. The sprites jumped into
the children with wicked glee and sent them laughing-
mad too. There was nothing funny any longer! It was
just wild, uncontrollable laughing. I jammed the food
back into the basket, hardly able to control my move-
ments and fled out of that temple down a grassy hill-
side, the children following and screaming behind me
and when we got to the bottom we lay on the grass
looking up at the sky until we recovered.

Then Stella, sitting up said:

"Wee lads! Look at that." We all sat up and looked at the hill in front of us, covered in broad, stone stairs, which led nowhere except up into the sky. Back we were thrust into the fairy-tale world—we might climb into another country where Jack-the-Giant-Killer dwelt. The children ran backwards and forwards along the length of each stair until we reached the top, then we sat down and looked around. Opposite us and on the same level, stood another hill with a martello tower on top. So down the stairway we went and up the hill to enter still another world. We sat down with our backs against the grim tower where an icy salt-wind was blowing off the choppy green sea and we looked across Bantry Bay towards the open Atlantic ocean. Here the atmosphere was of smugglers, pirates, shipwrecks, mutinies and the like. " 'Tis perishing up here," Timmy said with chattering teeth, shoulders humped and rubbing his hands. "We'll go down, will we?"

He looked so miserable we all got up and set off down the hill and came to a stop at a heavily studded garden door set in a stone wall; we tentatively opened it and stepped into the kitchen garden, then we walked along the neat paths bordered by bare gnarled fig-trees, resembling heavy wrought iron; other fruit trees filligreed the surrounding high walls. The garden was all made up of square and oblong patches enclosed inside wooden frames and the soil was covered thickly with brown pine needles. Each vegetable looked symmetrical and exotic—no maggot would dare trespass into such perfection!

The sun was shining here, too, but so unlike the first garden we had been through. This was real autumn sun, bright, barely warm, and full of mystery. The air smelt of michaelmas daisies, aromatic culinary herbs and burning leaves. Gardeners were silently sweeping the paths with twig-brooms and tending to their smoky fires and taking no notice of us. We went out at the far door and stood under a gigantic spreading tree covered with cones the size of pineapples, some of which had fallen on the spongy turf underneath. I popped one into the basket so that we could examine it when we got home, to make sure that we hadn't been dreaming.

The boatman was waiting to take us back to the mainland where the driver was standing by his car ready to take us back home and to reality.

37 THE STORM

THE sky was preparing for some big event! Thin, smoky clouds were stretching out their arms and joining up with rolling black masses, all was urgent hurry and scurry above, and beneath, the earth stood dark sullen and still. The animals had sensed something in the air and had hidden themselves away. We would have to get them all shut in before the storm began, so while Timmy and Stella cut ropefuls of green ferns to put in the cow-house for bedding, Mary, Joey and I went in search of them. We found Darky right down in the hazel copse near the strand; her eyes startled with fear gazed at us through the branches, and although Lassie barked and bit her tail, she refused to budge from the sheltered spot she had found for herself.

After a lot of prodding and whacking, she at last ran out but, determined to pay us back for moving her, she ran in every direction except on the track to the house. Lassie nearly went mad.

As soon as we had shut her in we went off again in search of the donkeys. They were well able to look after themselves but we were thinking of the foal. We found them in the big woods near the sea—their favourite place. When we drove them out on to the strand, they turned skittish and grabbed up pieces of seaweed and bit each other on the neck. They didn't sense the gloom that lay over the water and they hated being shut into the cow-house.

Diamond, Paddy's piebald pony, had backed into the turf-shed and was moving its rump backwards and forwards to try and get further in, so she was soon dealt with. The pet lamb wasn't far away either. The cow-house had a rich smell of ferns and animals and the dim green light in there made the cow look extra black and the lamb very white. Diamond stood in the far corner, not wishing to be mixed up with the rabble. Swallows dipped and darted in and out of the broken panes to their nests in the rafters.

As we were latching the cow-house door, the storm broke, and we ran for the house with our heads down, and barred the back door against the wind. We built up the fire into a huge blaze and pulled the seat up to it, but we couldn't concentrate on our books, we only listened to the rain peppering at the window like steel pellets, and to the rattle of the back door. We all went to bed early but I couldn't sleep. Thunder rumbled continuously round and round the mountain and wild fire lit up the room every second; I could see it even though my eyes were shut. The force of the storm was all concentrated on the back of the house which made it possible for me to have the front window wide open. I might have enjoyed listening to the wild fury outside if I hadn't been worrying about the hens up the hawthorn tree. It was their own fault, there was a perfectly good hen-house. I tried to comfort myself, thinking that they must be hardy by now and I piled the blankets round my head and went into some sort of coma which wasn't sleep. I was in this state for about an hour when I had a visitor—one that wakened me violently.

It was the storm itself! It burst open the bedroom door and entered my room in full gale force and in a flash and, with deft fingers, it picked up my heavy quilt and bundled it out of the window. I leapt out of bed and shut it out but before I was back into bed it had burst in again. A tornado was coming up the stairs which were acting as a funnel. I battled through it to find the back door wide open and the bolt snapped in two. I was freezing cold and I was getting soaked through by the rain driving in on me so I said, "To hell with the door!" and ran back to bed pushing a chest of drawers against my door. Then I lay listening to the stream roaring in flood and to the windows wheezing as though they were going to splinter in, and to the chimney rocking. This time I fell right off to sleep with the storm still gaining strength.

The next morning Timmy was the first to get up, "Janey Mack!" he shouted. "Come quick and look at the kitchen." His tone of voice sent us all rushing down the stairs.

"Oh boys, oh boys!" they all shouted, rolling up their pyjama legs and splashing through the water that was a foot up the walls in the kitchen and the room.

"Let's go and have a look at the stream," I said.

We all went out, game for anything after this. The wind was so strong we had to bend double and press with all our force to get along, and however hard we shouted we couldn't make ourselves heard. The bridge had been swept away by what was now a broad, swiftly flowing river instead of a small stream. It spread out over the fields at both sides and was trying to tear the lower branches off the sally trees which were festooned with yellow froth—like that on the top of ale. The wind was stretching the froth out like elastic and blowing it off in lumps and it went whizzing down the torrent at a hundred miles an hour.

"Let's bathe in it," I yelled with all my might.

I stripped off and stood on the very edge of the water and it came at me with such force it sprayed over my head leaving my front quite dry. The children soon followed suit and we were soon fiery red with the battering of the water. Then we ran about the fields, feeling as wild as the wind. We exhausted ourselves and went back into the house and prepared to rid it of the water. We worked all the morning with buckets and brooms. We could hardly recognize the cement floor in the kitchen, it was so clean and embedded with bright pebbles like a coloured mosaic.

By the late afternoon the storm was spent, the wind had dropped and the stream was shrinking to within its banks, leaving behind it flat, bedraggled grass. A thick mist lay over the sea and the birds were hopping about stiffly chirruping in a minor key.

I went to look for my quilt and found it lying in a heap at the bottom of the field—the red dye soaked into the white side. It must have floated through the air like a magic carpet for twenty yards.

38 I BUY A COW

Darky calved a red heifer and it will always remain a mystery where she got it from as there was no red bull within a twenty mile radius, unless, of course, she had met a wanderer like herself during that three days absence. It was such a fine calf that everyone wanted to buy it—I sold it to a neighbour for a good price but it proved to be a bad bargain. It grew and grew until it surpassed its utility as a milking cow and it had to be sold to the butcher for meat at half the price.

We sold Darky because she was such a big cow she took too much feeding, and as she was ten years old, she hadn't many years left for giving calves. So once more we found ourselves without a cow. I was weeding turnips when John Crahoore called to see me. "I hear tell, Ma'am, that ye are wantin' a cow. I was thinkin' would ye take a look at my animals before ye go te the fair temorrar." There was no harm in looking at them so that evening I walked up the mountain with Lassie and found John in a dark cabin, milking.

"I'll be out te ye in a minute, Ma'am. Then ye can take a look at this little cooby I'm just after milkin'." He led out a small Kerry cow. "Now this is the animal that'll suit ye, Ma'am, she's a fine cow without a fault in the world, God bless her!"

"Is that all the milk she gives?" I said, looking into the sweet-gallon only a quarter full.

"Yerra! ye can't ixpict more in the avinin', now in the mornin's she spills it over the rim, faith, and she's

166

not brittle neither—a child could milk her. She have
a nice maiden calf, ye can see her fer yerself," he said,
walking over to another small cabin.

"What are you asking for the two of them?" I said,
admiring the doe-like calf.

"Will, Ma'am, they're worth ivery pinny uf £16 and
that's givin' thim te ye chape, faith!"

"I can't go that high. I must find one for £12 or £13
at the most."

"Yerra malaire!" he said, putting away my offer with
his hand.

"Let me see any others you have."

"I will, I will indade, Ma'am," he said cheering up.
"Now there's a nate little animal," pointing to a yellow
polly over in the field, "she a shanafuch, calving iny
day from this off."

"But no one will buy polly cows," I said.

"Well, Ma'am, some of thim don't, thin more of thim
do. Perhaps ye've heard till that thim with the horns
is not always the bist milkers."

Just as he was saying this a cow with the heaviest
horns I had ever seen came lumbering towards us.

"Now there's a nice quiet animal, God bless her!"
he said.

The cow, catching sight of Lassie, lowered its head
and went for her, and although it barely touched her,
she being such a timid dog ran away yelping as though
she was hurt.

"'Tis the strange dog, yerra!" he said, after the com-
motion had died down.

As he had no more cows I told him that before I
decided I would have a look round the fair tomorrow.

"Thim fairs is a cod arou! Don't they take their
faulty animals there te get rid of thim? What else?

Who's going te take a good cow when they can make
good use uf it thimselves? Ye'll be sorry, Ma'am, if ye
don't strike a bargain wit me now, fer mine is proved
animals, ivery one uf thim, and I wouldn't be sellin'
at all but the rheumatics have me destroyed."

The next day I set off very early to the fair. Paddy
was staying away from us on one of his huffs, so for
the first time I had to buy an animal on my own. I
had just lifted my bike up on top of the Protestant
church-yard wall when a little man with a long stick
came up to me and asked if I wanted to buy a cow—
how he knew I don't know as women never did the
buying or selling of animals. He led me through the
town to the bottom of Main Street to take a look at
two "nate little springers."

I liked them immediately but it took me some time
to decide which one of them to have. They were both
the same price, £13, and they were both about to calf.
As soon as I decided, the little man said he would see
me through the town with her. At the top of the Bell
Height he left me and I went to lift my bike off the
wall. The cow must have thought no one was with her
because she turned and started galloping back into the
town.

As I passed Gow's shop someone shouted, "I see
ye've made a deal, Ma'am."

"I have but I can't catch it," I shouted back as I ran.

"Help the Missus with her cow, sonny," he shouted
to a young lad leading a whole group of heifers.

The boy caught my cow and she joined up with the
others and walked along quietly enough. When we
reached the pier cottages, the boy turned off and giving
my cow a whack along the road, he said I'd be all
right now. The cow jog-trotted along, then without

any warning turned and began to gallop back into
the town again. I flung my bike down and jumped in
front of her holding out my arms and doing foot-work
to equal any matador. The cow lowered her head and
for some time we blocked the traffic but she got past me
in the end. Willa Murt was coming over the crest of
the Bell Height and I shouted, "Stop her quick!" He
was wheeling his bike loaded up with long springy
planks. He turned the handle-bars, the planks shuddered and bobbed blocking most of the road and the
cow stopped. Then we set off again, down the Bell
Height, past the pier cottages and along the straight
stretch of road by the sea, Willa Murt and I chatting
away quite unconcernedly now that all was well. Then
just before we came to the bridge, there were two
up-ended rocks leaning outwards allowing just enough
room for a man to go through and she made a dash for
this opening, but jumping to clear the wide part, it mis-
calculated and sank down and stuck fast. She coughed,
her sides contracted, and she sank even lower. I said
good-bye to my £13. Together we pushed her with our
feet, shouted at her to "Git outa that" and whacked
her, but she did nothing to help herself. Willa Murt
had a piece of rope which he tied round her horns and
I went into the field and tugged at her with all my
strength while he, with his hands on the two rocks,
heaved at her with his shoulder, and at last with
another cough, she contracted and fell out into the
field and galloped off towards the sea. Willa Murt
opened the gate while I ran after her—she made
straight for the small gap again, but this time she leapt
right over the top of it. Once more we had her under
control and we walked over the bridge. At the boat-
house Willa Murt was going to repair a boat and had

to leave me. "Ye'll be all right now with the straight
road ahead o' ye," he said.

The only turning was the old road a mile further on
and it wouldn't matter if she did go that way so I
jumped on my bike and cycled slowly behind her as
she walked calmly along. Then without any warning
she jumped into the wood and started crashing about
in the thick growth there. I ran after her—at least I
stumbled and leapt and dragged my clothes away
from the thorny brambles and fell over fallen branches
and disappeared in deep bracken until I got so hot I
tore off my coat and flung it down. I was just in time
to see her reach the narrow path by the sea and turn
right and gallop towards the town. I was almost in
tears with anger and desperation when I saw someone
standing up on the low wall and peering through the
branches at me. Then the familiar voice of Jim Doyle
shouted, "Is that ye, Harry girral? and what arou doin'
at all leppin' around in the wood like a rabbit, faith?"
I explained and he said, "Let ye get out on to the road,
a hilla! and I'll see te yer cow." After looking all over
for my coat that I had left behind I at last came out
on to the road. My clothes were sticking to me with
sweat and my heart was beating in my temples. "Ye're
as hot as a young filly after a race, yerra," Jim Doyle
said. The cow seemed to know that there was a man
behind her and she caused no more trouble. As Jim
was shutting her into the cow-house, he said:

"Ye made a bad bargain with that one, begad! She's
wild out, yerra!"

39 INDOOR GAMES

FOR a brief second the sun would race from behind the blanket of grey cloud as though it were escaping from a dark prison and it would be a revelation! Everywhere would glow with colour. "Hi!" I'd shout up welcoming it after so many weeks' absence. Then invisible hands would tug it quickly back and we would be in the gloom again that lay like lead over us. The rain would pelt down as though it were trying to obliterate our memory of the recent bit of sun.

The children, who were on holiday, were forced to play indoors not that they minded bad weather usually but this time it was impossible to walk, even in the fields, because they were like wet sponges filled to their capacity. The water ran over our feet with every step, wheezing and squelching in protest—I shovelled the mud away from the path up to the cow-house but it slithered silently back as soon as my back was turned. The sea would surely gulp up this dead weight of an Ireland, I began to think!

The children invented games to play indoors and one of them they called 'Whale'. The floor was the sea and the three beds were the ships where the passengers were forced to leap about to escape the clutches of the whale who tried to grab them by the ankle and drag them under. This game began by everyone stripping off down to their vests and pants because, although both windows at either side of the room were wide open, the players still got flaming hot with all the

171

energy they put into it. Whale had to keep his jersey on all the time because he had to lie on his back and shoot from one side of the room to the other. He would start by doubling his knees up to his chin and gripping one of the bed-rails to ensure a good push off on the floor that was like glass. When he heard the word 'ready' then whale would shoot back and forth like a shuttle-cock. To choose the first whale, they said this piece of poetry:

> *When I climbed up the apple tree,*
> *All the apples fell on me.*
> *Make a cake, make a pie,*
> *Take it round to Hannah Marri,*
> *Hannah Marri isn't in, so take it*
> * round to Lizzy Flynn.*
> *Each a peach, a pear, a plum,*
> *Out goes my very best chum.*

They made so much noise at this game that people used often to come down from the old road to see if they were all right. They invented a cooling-off game called 'Post Offices', each one taking over a corner of the room with the telephone numbers written on the wall beside them and imitating the girl in the Post Office in Kenmare who had a permanent cold, they'd say:

"Hillo, hillo, is dat ye, Killardy? I have a bessage fer ye, Killardy, if yer ready."

There was no definite structure to this game; it kept going off at a tangent.

"Oh, hillo, is dat ye, Jack?" one of them would reply.

" 'Tis me all right, Jack,"—they all shared the name 'Jack'.

"Will ye come over te my house fer tea, Jack? I'll ring up and tell ye whin I'm ready fer ye."

Then they would leave their corners and go visiting.

"Oh, hillo, Jack, tie ye horse up outside and come on inside."

"How's ye baby, Jack?" one of them would ask and a nonsensical conversation would go on until they went back to their corners and began the ringing up again.

" 'Tis not yer turn to ring up."

" 'Tis so."

" 'Tis not."

" 'Tis shot."

"Ye were first yisterday."

" 'Twas ere yisterday."

" 'Twas in my eye!"

I would interrupt at this point by bawling "Tea!" and they would come rushing down the stairs as though they had never had a meal in their lives and place themselves at the table in their usual positions. Mary sat on her feet, Joey stood up on her chair, Timmy knelt on his, and Stella sprawled sideways with her back against the wall. They looked so terrible I made a drawing of them and when I showed it to them they laughed so much that Stella began to slide down the wall until she landed on the cement floor with her mug broken to pieces and a pool of tea all round her, which made everyone laugh more than ever. As soon as the tea was cleared away they played 'Circuses'. They dressed Lassie and the cat in head scarves and skirts and made them jump through their hoops. Lassie didn't quite know what she was supposed to do and twisted about, drooling at the mouth and grinning with excitement until she had to be put out of the room in case she had another fit. The cat's eyes were dilated with fear and she scratched so much she had to be put out too. Then they had to be their own animals, monkeys jumping up on the furniture, scratching and chattering, or seals balancing things on their noses or circus ponies running round and round the room on each other's backs. On one of these occasions, Stella fell and lay giggling for so long that I thought she was going into hysterics but instead of slapping her face as one is supposed to do, I said, "Don't be such an idiot and get up, you ass." I said it harshly enough but it failed to get her on to her feet and in the end we discovered that she had broken her leg. Fortunately—or perhaps it wasn't fortunate—Paddy was there that evening and he took her into Kenmare on the bar of his bike, and leaving her at his mother's house, he went off in search of the doctor and eventually found him in the cinema. He came rushing out and into Paddy's mother's like a whirl-wind swearing and cursing because he was missing the news and roaring and laughing because he had hit someone in the bloody belly on the way out. Irish doctors, I had come to the conclusion, were of quite a different breed to the English ones who take themselves so seriously. He tied a piece of rag round her leg and as he ran back to the news, shouted that he'd see her in the morning. She might as well have stayed at home. For the next few weeks Stella went around with two broom tops under her arms until her leg healed.

To get back to the games: they took turns in being the ring-master with the whip.

"Stop it, ye're hurting," someone would complain, "I won't play if ye're going to hit so hard."

"Hard my foot! When *ye* had the whip, didn't ye make Joey cry?"

"Huh! Doesn't she cry for nothing?"

"Let's play 'My Ship Sails'" Stella would say, interrupting the argument.

"Ou ya! Bags choose the first letter," they'd all shout together and another rhyme would have to be gone through to make it fair. The letter chosen was "W" and Timmy began.

"My ship sails laden wit Wiolins".

"Violins, you ejet! That's 'V'."

So he was allowed another turn but it was just as bad; his next word was 'Wollinteers'.

"Oh, it's hopeless playing this game. We'll play 'Coffee Pot' instead," Stella said.

The game was to choose a word with more than one meaning such as 'flower' and 'flour' and when they were asked questions they had to answer bringing in their word but changing it to the word 'coffee pot'.

Mary thought of the first word and we guessed for so long we had to give in.

"'Tis 'tree' one, two, *tree*, and tree that grows."

We gave her another chance and again we couldn't guess it.

"'Tis taught' to teach and 'taut' to tink."

"It's not fair," Joey grumbled, "ye niver let me have a turn."

"Oh, all right then," Stella said impatiently, "I've got a word now you ask *me* a question."

Joey thought and thought.

"Hurry on," Stella said impatiently.

"But I don't know what to ask," Joey said, delighted that all the attention was on her.

"Anything, anything at all, just say the first thing that comes into your head."

After another long silence, she suddenly brightened and said, "Pipey."

When everyone had recovered from laughing, they said,

"What's Pipey anyway?"

"How do I know," she said, "Stella told me to say *anything*."

"I know! Let Harry ask us questions for pennies," Mary would suggest.

They had often played this game and ought to have known the answers off by heart.

"Who is the Prime Minister of England?" I asked Timmy.

"Mick-the-Pig," he replied.

"He means 'John-the-Bull'," Mary said scornfully.

"Who's the head of Italy?"

"Mona Lisa", she said slickly.

Mussolini, I corrected her. "Well there's hardly any difference," she said, as though I were being too fussy.

"Mary," I went on, "who is the head of the government in Ireland?"

"Leonado de Vinci." "'Tis near enough," she said when I told her De Valera.

"I'm either a rotten teacher or else you are a lot of egits," I said. "Timmy, you name six insects."

"A doldare, a guilshook, a troomplan, a skritarn, a slater and a pig."

He explained what each one was and I had to give him a penny.

"Now Mary, you name six birds, and in English this time."

"Norry-the-bogs, garkers, squarl-crows, a wrin, a gowreen and a sparra."

"It's no fun playing these games, let's play "Concerts", Stella said.

They all got on top of Bridie's flour chest and sang 'The Maid of County Down' and as usual the words were wrong.

> *Such a croaky elf I had to choke myself*
> *To make shure I was really there.*

Then Stella sang "At sixty-three I fell in love quite madly."

"Twenty-three, you oaf!" I corrected.

"Don't be always interrupting. What difference does it make anyway?" she complained.

Perhaps none at all, I thought.

40 THE PICTURES

THERE was always some entertainment going on in Kenmare. The pictures were on all the year round and during the winter months the Carnegie Hall was booked for Anew McMaster who came three times a year, playing Shakespeare, Oedipus Rex and other good plays. A Spanish company called the De Gabriels came in between times with musical shows and the local talent came on to the boards whenever it could be squeezed in.

I preferred the plays but the children liked the pictures. Tomorrow evening there was going to be a Tarzan film and they wouldn't miss one of these, not for anything! I promised to take them because Joey wanted to go, and she was a nuisance when she got tired and had to be carried. But when the time came there was a storm raging so I naturally thought the arrangement was off.

"We won't melt," Mary said crossly.

"Haven't we our macs and wellingtons and everything," Timmy went on petulantly.

"You promised." 'Try and get out of that one,' was in the tone of Stella's voice.

"And if you don't keep it we'll never believe ye again," said Mary, picking up this strong line.

I shouldn't have listened to them—I was as crazy as they were not to have put my foot down immediately, instead I reluctantly got ready. But no sooner were we over the door-step than I regretted it.

A blast of rain-laden wind hit us like a sledge-hammer, straining the tapes on our sou-westers against our necks and nearly choking us. Our capes rattled up over our heads and we had to hold them down with both hands from the inside. The path down to the line was all wet slithery mud and we couldn't see a hand in front of us; the rain ran off our capes into the tops of our wellingtons and by the time we reached the road we were all wet through. Then I suggested that we turned back—"But we've got over the worst part" —"We may be wet but we're warm," and suchlike pronouncements drove us onwards, splashing through lakes of water that flooded the road, until we came to the woods, and there we were brought to a halt by a fallen tree lying across our path.

It was then I again suggested turning back. *I* could if I liked but they were going on, now that they had got that far. The night was so wild I was afraid to let them go on alone so we started to climb through the branches of the tree. Pine-needles slashed across our faces, our capes hooked on to broken twigs and we slipped and grazed our knees. Joey started to scream and I got hold of her hand and dragged her after me. In the end we cleared the tree but immediately came to another and then a third one. To think of going through this gruelling nightmare just to see a film was ludicrous! But on we went arriving at the cinema half an hour late to find that there were no seats left except a few that were under a leaky part of the roof.

Of course as we had got that far we went in and sat down in the sodden plush with drips falling on us in uneven spurts. Watching Boy and the Maureen girl and Tarzan leaping in and out of a water-hole didn't distract us very much from our own discomforts.

There came a loud explosion of thunder—the film snapped and the lights fused and we were thrust into darkness. After ten minutes of listening to the children in the fourpennies bawling and screeching, someone with a torch got up on to the platform and apologised for the breakdown and said they were unable to repair it and that our money would be refunded at the door on the way out and the same film would be showing the following evening. We filed out in the dark to a rasping gramophone record playing 'If you're up to your eyes in hot water just be like the kettle and sing'. What I said when I got out, even this book would throw out of its pages!

41 THE DUCK AND DRAKE

In the kitchen the log and turf fire was blazing up the wide chimney, and outside, big, fleecy snowflakes were being blown in a whirling maze in every direction. Only the near things were visible such as turf-hen- and cow-houses which looked like dirty hovels under their thick snow-covered roofs. The stiff frozen leaves of the palm tree were clacking in the wind and the branches of the monkey puzzle tree were swaying up and down covered with thick wads of snow.

Mary and Timmy had only seen snow in the distance on the tops of the mountains so they couldn't stop gazing out of the window, and as there hadn't been a fall of snow in Kerry for thirty years, they weren't the only ones to be excited. The Kenmare children had to be kept indoors because it was unsafe for them to be out on the streets as the shop-keepers had built walls of snow on the pavements and were pelting snowballs at one another all through the day and night.

Even the animals acted peculiarly. When we let the cow out, she pranced about playfully biting up the snow and the dogs prowled like wolves, killing the sheep that were caught in the drifts. When they were caught in the act they were shot and hung up on a tree as a warning to other dogs that might be tempted to do the same.

As we were looking out of the window we noticed the broody hen sitting on top of the wall with her feathers being blown inside out. Timmy put a coat over his head and went out to see what she was doing there and we watched him lift her down off the wall and put three eggs into his pocket, but no sooner was he in the house than she had jumped up again. She pulled some loose stones under her and made them as hot as eggs and there she would have sat for ever if I hadn't thought of an idea. I had heard Mrs Sullivan say that chickens would perish in the winter but ducklings were hardy and could survive the bad weather, so we went along to Tommy-the-Points to buy some of his duck eggs. I had often admired his ducks because they seemed to enjoy life to the full. They lived on the strand and ate whatever sea-food they could forage; this made their eggs taste of fish, which one grew to like after a time. They had low timber shelters on the banks where they laid their eggs, but more often they laid them in the sea and the tide washed them up. They were always flying through the spray low over the waves and were undistinguishable from wild ducks. We brought back twelve green eggs and put every one under the broody-hen, thinking that we would take away the ones she wasn't able to cover but she clawed them and rolled them under her with her beak and shuffled her body about until every one disappeared and she sat looking twice her normal size— a great buxom mother-hen! Timmy built a house over her and put a big rock on the roof to hold it down during the storms. She wouldn't budge; we had to carry food to her.

After four weeks twelve yellow fluff balls tumbled off the wall following their foster-mother. The children sank a big dish into a hole in the ground and filled it up with water for the ducklings and they flopped in and out of it all day long, to the consternation of the hen. When they grew bigger and discovered the stream, this proved too much for the hen. She ran backwards and forwards along the bank calling them to come out and of course they took no notice. She soon lost her fat, motherly appearance and turned into a scraggy bird with limp, greasy feathers hanging from her. Not only did it ruin her character but it perverted the ducks too.

Then one morning Mary came in carrying a dead duckling, its head twisted round on to its back and its beak gaping open, and all that day we kept finding more, all having died the same way. Mrs Sullivan thought that they must have choked from eating the pony's oats. Out of the twelve, only two survived, a duck and a drake. The duck grew up to be common, fat, an ordinary fawn colour with a raucous quack and an exaggerated waddle, but she was good natured and lovable—she always looked as though she were smiling. The drake was of quite a different calibre; he was an aristocrat, a rake and a devil. His colouring was of the palest fawn with wing feathers and head of metallic-green and cutely curled white tail feathers. His legs and beak were marigold yellow and his eyes were like dull black old-fashioned boot-buttons. He had one big vice. He lusted after the hens and his technique was highly developed. He and the duck would stand on the out-side ring of hens and with his dull, devilish eyes he would pick out his fancy. As soon as the decision was made he would waste no more time but rush straight at her and knock her about roughly with his head and tweak at her feathers. This went on until the hen, realizing what was happening, would let out a terrified squawk. This made him immediately alter his tactics; he would stop the rough stuff and start running round and round her in a close circle while she would nearly wring her own neck trying to watch him. When she was thoroughly mesmerized, and dizzy, he did as he liked.

Agonizing squawks rent the air when she came-to again and there was no stopping her this time. The cock would immediately leave off whatever he was doing and would stand erect, listening, with his eyes on fire and his tail feathers stiffly arched like the statue of 'Coq D'or'.

Then with head down he would come striding to her rescue and peck the drake deep into his neck, sending him off waggling his tail feathers with pain and watch him poised like a warrior with drake's blood hanging in a crimson drop from his beak. The drake, looking foolishly embarrassed, would join the benevolently smiling duck, and they would waddle off together up to the deep pool under the bridge.

But the time came when the drake had entirely his own way and however much the hens called for help, the cock took no notice; he couldn't he was too ill; he was moulting! All day he would stand moping under the shade of the fuchsia hedge, his once fiery comb now drooping and purple, his ashen eyelids closed up over his dull sick eyes and his tatty feathers hanging off him, tipping the ground. He was no longer their Lord and Master!

The duck had only one big interest and that was the drake. So that she needn't spend any time away from him she laid her eggs in the water and we used to collect them caught between the rocks. But once she decided to hatch out some of her eggs. We couldn't think where she had got to, we searched everywhere. The drake helped to pull the undergrowth away from the hedge bottom with his beak and when a hole was made he would call urgently and listen for a reply. Then we found her sitting smug and silent in the middle of a clump of ragwort.

As soon as he knew where she was he wouldn't leave her alone; he just couldn't understand it at all, especially when the food was put out on the grass and she refused to budge. He wouldn't eat any of it himself, only run round and round keeping it from the hens in case she should turn up. Later on when she did leave her nest to feed he kept all the hens off in the same way until she had eaten her fill. I never once saw him eat the whole time the duck was sitting. He was a gallant drake then! But she soon began to realize that her life was by drake's side and her half-hatched eggs were abandoned and once more they were together copulating all day long in the deep pool under the bridge.

He was so pleased at her reappearance that he acted the fool. One day I really thought his high spirits had gone a bit far. We were all standing on top of the hill in the front and he soared up into the air as high as the house and the duck put her head on the side and watched him with one black eye—of course it may have been a gust of wind that took him but when he began to veer sideways we thought he was off to join the wild ducks down by the sea, but he sank down again and, waggling with pride, he looked at the duck as much as to say "That was a bit of all right, eh?"

Some weeks after this I was wakened in the middle of the night by the drake running round and round the house and calling urgently and I knew something must have happened to the duck. It would have been useless my getting up as it was so dark, but first thing in the morning, as the drake was still calling, I went out and together we searched the fields and hedges. He waddled after me everywhere I went, calling continuously, and as we were walking up from the road, I saw a fawn feather lying beside a boulder and when I looked behind it I saw a ring of pale down on the grass, and there was a smell of fox.

Naturally, I abandoned the search but, not so, the drake. All day he poked his head into the hedges calling her to come out until I couldn't bear it any longer. I put him in a bag and carried him along to Tommy-the-Point's and put him down on the edge of the sea and ran away hoping that he would forget, and fly in the spray like the others, and like the others be carefree and gay.

THE children came back from the fair full of excitement as they always did after every fair. This time, they had seen a man in the street with a performing monkey, and none of them had ever seen one before. Cissy-May in the shop had given Timmy an ice-cream for nothing and he had gone so red that they were all teasing him. Before long "Timmy loves Cissy-May" filled every available space on the walls. Every incident was recorded on the walls in writing and drawings. Stella drew horses and Joey brides. They had watched a wedding—the first one they had ever seen—in Kenmare and they were so impressed they never tired of drawing it.

Everyone at the fair had been remarking about what a fine girl Mary was growing into. She was fourteen, had straight black hair, big grey eyes and a flawless complexion. As she had never looked better, I didn't take much notice when she complained of a pain in her jaw, even when she stayed in bed the following day, because she was sitting up, knitting, and eating huge meals and as she was a lazy girl this might be a stunt to avoid the work. But after three days it was becoming a joke. "Come down, Miss Connor [after the woman who had shut herself in at Connor's Corner] or will we board up the windows for ye?" they were shouting up to her. She laughed at this but still nothing would induce her to get up.

I went to the strand, leaving Mary looking well and

cheerful and within half-an-hour Stella came running
down to tell me that Mary felt ill. I dropped everything and came up to the house and asked her if she
would like me to get the doctor—she said she
would; so I set off to Kenmare on my bike—when
I had got only a short way along the road I remembered
I had left my watch on top of a rock and if I left it
until I came back the tide would take it. So I flew back
and when I reached the strand I saw that a wave was
lapping right up to the top of the rock. I walked into
the sea in my clothes and grabbed it. The next wave
flowed over the rock. I did so much running about
after this that my clothes soon dried. The doctor had
been seen going to play golf so I ran from green to
green asking everyone if they had seen him but he was
always "just ahead." In the end I had to leave a
message for him to come up as soon as possible.

He came the following morning but before he went
up to see Mary he played noisily with the children.
Then he rushed like a whirlwind into her bedroom and
the minute he saw her his face changed. She had
meningitis, but I wasn't to worry unduly. He had some
tablets—the latest invention—that would cure her
within a few days. Every five hours she had to have
two crushed in water. In three days she was well and
wanted to get up. As it was hot sunny weather I let
her sit at the back door, putting the clothes-horse
draped with rugs, round her to keep out any draughts.
She enjoyed watching the chickens cheeping around
her feet, and for the next three days she was up and
down, resting in bed whenever she felt like it. On the
fourth day she wouldn't get up and I thought she must
have over-done it a little the day before, but when she
was still in bed in the afternoon I began to worry. In

the evening she said she felt awful so I went for the doctor again and he came up straight away this time. The minute he saw her he wrapped her up in her bed-clothes and carried her to his car. He was going to take her to the County Hospital in Kenmare he said. Mary and I sat in the back seat and she made a few feeble jokes and I laughed so that she wouldn't feel frightened.

The next morning I cycled in to the hospital and was horrified to see her unconcious, and the matron moaning and saying there was no hope of her recovery and that it was God's will. She repeated "'Tis God's will," so many times I could hardly resist slapping her in the face to stop her. I suggested taking her to the hospital in Cork if she thought that there was a chance of further treatment. She doubted it but one never knows. So with this faint hope I went off in search of the man in charge of the ambulance. When I at last found him he said he wasn't able to let me have it because I hadn't paid any subscription towards it.

Then seeing how worried I was he changed his mind and said I could have it but that there was no driver because it was Sunday. After combing the streets I eventually found one and arrived back at the hospital after nearly two hours' delay, only to find another set-back! Sticks was expected any minute and nothing could be done without his consent, as he was Mary's nearest relative. Then *they* gave in too, seeing the urgency of the situation, and just as we were going out through the gates, Sticks turned up. I was never so pleased to see anyone! And what a terrible journey that was! Mary lay unconscious looking just the same as she always looked when she was well—it was im-possible to believe that she was so ill. Sticks chain-smoked all the way, the ambulance rolled like a ship at sea, the windows were all shut, I was so dizzy I couldn't see straight and any minute I thought I was going to be sick. But we reached the hospital without my having to stop on the road. Mary was immediately taken in on a stretcher and Sticks and I were directed to another entrance. We had to pass through the main hall where some sort of religious ceremony was going on. Nuns in voluminous white habits, starched out to enormous proportions, filled every space and I had to push my way through this sea of starch, excusing myself all the time, but they were so engrossed they didn't seem to notice me, thank goodness. I was quicker than Sticks and I could see by the swaying of the white starch when he was about to surface. Mary was being examined by the doctor and we were shown into a small room. We hadn't long to wait; he came in looking very worried and asked Sticks and me all kinds of questions about her general health and heredity, adding that it was no use our waiting any longer; he would let us know how she progressed. We went back in the same ambulance but with all the windows open this time, but feeling much more depressed.

Sticks stayed at Killah overnight to await news from the hospital and early in the morning a telegram came to say that Mary had died in the night. Everything suddenly became unreal. The sun on the fields shone darkly, the vegetables growing in the garden looked foolish. Stella and Timmy, after I told them, continued with their game as though nothing had happened, and their laughter seemed to be echoing in a void.

In the afternoon we were in some misty, distant world—a world half comical, half sad. The house was full of people—all except us were crying.

They—the old women—kept saying to Timmy "The craythur! Is it missing yer sister ye are?" and he looked at them, smiling foolishly, and said he didn't and went on playing.

Joey's reactions were that she wished Mary would come back and bump her downstairs—a game they used to play.

I was trapped in the thought that it was my fault. If only I had taken her illness more seriously in the beginning. If I hadn't let her sit in the sun perhaps she would never have had a relapse, and maybe if she had been taken to Cork earlier she would have been cured. I blamed the doctor too; I should have *made* him come up more often, but he ought to have known better than I what to do. I couldn't speak or even look at the doctor, especially when later Patsy came over and I heard them laughing together. I know it was silly to feel this way, but at the time I couldn't help it.

When we heard that Patsy was coming we had to lime-wash all the walls in the house in case she would be disgusted at the drawings and writings and the general mess they were in.

All the years we had lived in Ireland the children had had to fine comb their hair every evening, but during Mary's illness we had all forgotten about it and when Patsy came, they were alive—she *was* disgusted after all.

Patsy and I had a long talk about Timmy's future. He was almost fourteen and soon he would be too old to attend the Boys' School. What did I think he was capable of doing? All I could think of was carpentry and Patsy didn't seem to think much of this as a career. He was always carving pieces of wood he found lying about the place and it seemed his one big interest then.

Patsy said he hadn't to be a vegetarian any longer and if he stayed on with me I would have to give him meat every day, and this I couldn't agree to. Then she thought that maybe if she took him back to England with her it would be better still. Although I didn't want him to go I was afraid now that something might happen to him, and also I knew that England had more facilities for teaching him a career. Patsy was staying at the Muxna Hotel and was due back in England the next day, and in the morning a small boy came up with a note from her to say that she had decided to take Timmy with her, and would I send him in and bring all his clothes. All of Timmy's clothes were on the line and it was pouring with rain so I half dried them in front of the fire and packed them into a case and set off hoping I would get a lift, but the road was deserted. My arms were nearly dragged out by the roots and my back ached and when I reached the hotel I was completely exhausted. Timmy was delighted to be going off to England. He wanted to see the aeroplanes and the bombing and when the time came for me to leave, he was more interested in switching the electric switches on and off than in saying good-bye to me.

I walked back in the rain, sobbing—not so much for my own sake but at the thought of Stella being left without Timmy. For all the six years we had lived together, they never went anywhere without saying, "Coming, Stella?" or "Coming, Timmy?" Timmy would be in a new place with new interests but Stella would be alone. Nearly all the young people who lived near us had gone off to America and only Nora-up-the-mountain was left, and she was going soon. What was I to do about Stella?

TIMMY wrote to us from England telling us about his school there and that he was learning French, and that he helped Aunty Patsy in the hotel when he was not at school and that he would be over to see us soon.

Stella was still at the convent and Joey at Dourus School.

One day two young men, strangers to Kenmare, were seen walking round the town and enquiring about empty rooms and asking all about the convent and the Boys' school. No one could think what their business was at all—then it all came out. They wanted to start a secondary school in Kenmare. They had already been to Killarney to ask for permission from the Bishop but he had refused to give it; the schools in Kenmare were good enough, he had said. But the young men weren't to be put off; they went ahead, looking for a suitable place and they tried to canvass pupils. If you were in the town you would see the young masters walking the streets all day with a few small boys at their heels. The numbers grew slowly but surely day by day until there were a dozen or so, but still no place where they could be taught, then, in the end, someone lent them a disused warehouse in the square. Everyone was curious, and there was a continual tramp up the dark, cobwebbed stairs to 'take a look at them'. This was disturbing enough but what was worse was the smell of fust and rats and the dim dust-ridden atmosphere, and after a few weeks they couldn't bear it any longer and were forced to move out so once again the masters and the boys were seen wandering the streets looking for a room. Then they were lent the Carnegie Hall for one week only while they looked for another place but at the end of the week they were on the streets again. At this point, Stella left the convent and joined the wandering scholars—she was the first girl but others soon followed until the numbers doubled.

There was an empty shop in Henry Street and they were given permission to move in. They carried chairs from the cinema each day and the counters seated the rest. There was no lavatory in the shop so they had to run all the way up to the railway station toilet, which took them about ten minutes each way. They ate their lunch sandwiches walking up and down the street and whenever anyone saw a child from the Secondary School they always imitated them munching.

It was found to be very interesting to watch the pupils through the plate glass windows having their lessons, but it was so distracting to the pupils that the windows had to be whitewashed. But they still had no peace because all the smaller children who were deprived of their peep-show banged with the palms of their hands on the glass, sing-songing, "Sec-on-derry-Schoo-al, Sec-on-derry-Schoo-al!" The masters would chase them away, but instead of giving them a slap, they only tickled them until they extracted a promise from them not to do it again. This was great fun and in the end every child in the town was banging on the windows and running in flocks down the street and jumping round screaming when any one of them was caught.

In the end their parents had to use stern methods to keep them away from the Secondary School. But even then there was still not much peace. The door-way was used for a shelter against the rain, and the various conversations that went on didn't mix very well with arithmetic or grammar lessons. The old men would talk away while everyone inside waited for them to stop.

"Baccy's scarce, faith,"

" 'Tis a fright altogether, yerra."

"But my son tells me that 'tis plintiful on the overan side."

"Shure there's whips uf it there."

Or an old woman would shout at the top of her voice to someone across the street, " 'Tis scrahauny owld wither."

Another day an old woman was tying her bootlace and leaning against the shop door. The door burst open sending her tumbling into the class, spilling a bag of flour all over the floor.

"God almighty and all above us! It have me destroyed, the bloody door, bad cess to it!" she blasphemed.

I used to look forward to Stella coming home in the evening to hear about the Secondary School; even the lessons were fun. The masters would juggle with the chalk while they were asking questions and if the answer wasn't correct they would throw the chalk at him, or, if they were near, swing the black-board on to his head. They joked with the children in an uninhibited and unprintable way, and the days passed with everyone enjoying every minute of the school. Then the Bishop made a pronouncement, and everything changed. If a certain percentage of children didn't pass some exam or other, he would close down the school. The masters bought canes and the fooling had to stop.

All the lessons had to be taught through the medium of Irish. Most of the children knew Irish from their parents but Stella didn't know any so she—out of boredom—became the naughty girl of the class. How could she sit still and learn Latin, Arithmetic, French and Algebra through Gaelic? She was always either being caned or else sent out on to the street. On one of these occasions she was told that she hadn't to come back unless she apologised, so she walked home. I went into town and had a talk with the masters and it ended by Stella leaving the school.

AFTER five years we were no longer strangers and instead of visitors coming to 'take a look at the foreign woman' and bringing gifts, the same people came but to borrow the scythe, the cross-cut or perhaps the broody hen, or else to ask for a load of ferns in exchange for a day's work. I was often asked to turn a skirt or make a smock, as I was the only one with a sewing machine. By now there was very little I wasn't able to do on the farm and it was as well because all the available men were conscripted to work at the Bog of Allen. All machinery and even the trains had to be fuelled with turf because the coal-boat sailed no longer up the Kenmare River with its bulging brown sails, bringing coal from Liverpool.

The shops sold fewer and fewer things as the war progressed. There was very little tea, no coffee, no fruit, neither dried nor fresh, no bicycle tyres; I had to go to town on the pony's back. (One day I went to town to buy a kettle and instead I came home with a pony which we called Shamrock because it had a patch of brown hair the shape of a shamrock on its otherwise white body.)

A coffee substitute called 'Cafe-o-Eire' was being sold in the shops and I was trying it for the first time when Mrs Sullivan came down so I asked her if she would like to try a cup of it, but warned her at the same time that it might make her sick.

"What harum!" she said, indignantly, "shure, haven't I the night long to throw it up!"

Whatever food we needed we had to grow ourselves or else do without. Everyone jumped off their bikes and horse-cars to watch us plant potatoes, cart manure, or throw lime over the land with a shovel.

"Ye're as good as iny man," they'd shout admiringly.

Bina-up-the-mountain helped us and even Joey had to work like the rest of us, but it was always fun and never drudgery. One day the government agricultural man called on his rounds to see if we wanted any advice about the crops and he took off his smart tweed coat and helped us second-earth the potatoes. We brought food down and had our meal sitting in the corner of the field and he said that my bread, made from wheat we had grown ourselves, was the best he had ever tasted; so I had improved since my bread-making lesson long ago.

The war was raging everwhere except in Ireland. Only one aeroplane ever came over Kerry and it circled round and round over the town and surrounding mountains striking panic into everyone who saw it. The Dourus school children hid under their desks screaming with terror, praying and crossing themselves. Bina-up-the-mountain was taking their donkey home when the plane zoomed over her head; she let go the donkey and ran as fast as her legs would carry her, falling over hummocks and up to her waist in bog-water; when she reached home another shock awaited her, her grandmother who had never left her bed for five years was walking down the fields praying with her rosary beads. Even the animals panicked, huddling into their cabins and trembling with fright.

England threatened to take the ports, and the Germans might land—in case this happened all the sign-posts were taken down and all the bridges were mined. The Home Guards were formed, and their first gun practice was in our fields below the road. Stella, mad with excitement, went running up to ask Mrs Sullivan what it was all about and she came back looking very crest-fallen. "What did she say?" I asked. "Oh, she just said that they were firin' farts and shootin' shits." It wasn't the answer she had wanted. The Home Guards had been robbed of their glory!

Another time the Home Guards came running in a body up to the house to capture the parachutists that had been seen landing on our strand. Again Stella was expecting something spectacular but was disappointed when it was discovered that the parachutists were nothing else but swathes of hay that had been caught up by the wind and carried across the sea inlet.

The next occurrence that caused excitement was over a couple that had taken the haunted house on the road to Kenmare which hadn't been lived in for years. They were both young, and English, and everyone was conjecturing as to how they were able to get out of England in the middle of the war when even Irish people had difficulty in doing so. What was their business in Kenmare? Were they spies and if not, then why did they go walking in the middle of the night? "Been fishing," they said to the Home Guards when questioned. "But we know better," everyone said, "no fish and no line; we're not daft."

"And what were they doing on top of Moll's Gap lighting flares at two o'clock in the morning?"

"Taking a rest and lighting a pipe and a cigarette, after walking back from the theatre in Killarney," they said.

Lies, lies, they told nothing but lies, a different story

to each one. It was maddening to say the least of it, not to know exactly what their business was. The few people that had been inside of their house said that it was full of locked trunks. 'Silver-ware' they said they contained, but 'wireless transmitters' said everyone else. They would take turns in going away for a week or two at a stretch, "to visit a dentist" they said; "to get instructions" said everyone else.

We had two cows now so that when one ran dry, we would be kept supplied with milk and butter from the other one. The little foal was now a fully grown donkey, but like its mother, not strong enough for all the heavy work. The other two donkeys, Patta and Mara, were both in foal again. Lassie was the only one who wasn't 'increasing our store'. She never had pups because she was scared to death of every dog that came near her. Instead of "May God incrase ye store, Ma'am," as the tinker boy had wished us, I was begining to think that their curse, "May the grass grow green under yer door," would be more of a blessing. We couldn't keep pace with the rate that everything was increasing, especially the hens hatching chickens out by the hundreds, all descendants of the six hens Mrs Sullivan had given us when we first came. With being so inter-bred, they were turning out freaks. "Carboons" Mrs Sullivan called them, sexless birds that would never be able to lay an egg and their only use was for the table and as we didn't eat them, that wasn't much consolation. I gave them to Bina-up-the-mountain's family and they said that they were the best they had ever eaten. "More doodle!" the youngest child shouted at the top of his voice after eating a piece of one of them, but I hoped that I wasn't going to be the one to supply him with more of those doodles. What's

more, they ate twice as much as any of the others and
hen-food was both dear and scarce. Their only virtue
was that they were easily caught because they were
always in the kitchen searching for more food.

Stella had learnt to play Irish reels on a melodeon
that I had bought for her and every Sunday afternoon
any young person that was around would come along
to dance to her playing.

We were all changing through the years. Stella was
in her rebellious teens. She wanted to see the world
but wasn't allowed to leave Ireland unless she was old
enough to do war-work. She and Bina-up-the-mountain rebelled together, probably having a fine time of
it, I don't know! All I knew was that I was worried
beyond words. I thought that Stella had T.B. because
she had such a cough; so bad that it resounded in my
own chest. They spent all their time in an old cowluck
up the mountain, smoking and fooling about. In
all weathers they were up there and Stella refused to
change her wet clothes when she came in. I don't know
whether it was this or smoking or a combination of the
two that gave her the cough. She laughed when I
suggested that she should see a doctor. I couldn't drag
her there against her will—she was bigger than I—so
what could I do but look on and hope she wasn't as
bad as she looked and sounded?

She was as wild as a mountain-goat and with
much less sense. Her mass of tangled red hair forgot
what a comb looked like and her wan, pale face never
had a chance to show its true colour through the dirt.
Perhaps I'd have got more of a shock if it had.

Then something of little importance happened but
whose influence was enormous, and it sowed the final
seeds of discontent. 'The Radio Stars' came from

Dublin with a revue. That kind of show had never been seen in Kenmare before. The old men objected, "We want none o' them high-brows comin' here," they said, "give us Willy Shakespeare like we're used to, faith." But they came, "girls with an inch of material between them and decency" singing the latest hit tunes and acting in suggestive sketches in dresses barely covering "their pelts." The priests tried to have the shows stopped but they didn't succeed. The Radio Stars stayed for their allotted time—two whole weeks, and Stella and Bina went every single night. Where Stella got the money from, I don't know to this day as I only gave her enough to go every other night. As it didn't finish until one thirty I thought the late nights would injure her health still further. These people represented the big world to Stella and after they had gone she became so unsettled that I knew we would have to move, but where? The answer came—not the right one but I clutched at it like someone drowning. I met a woman in Kenmare, she was a native of Buncrana in County Donegal and her description of her home town sounded almost as pleasant a place to live as Kenmare so I decided to go there. The children would be able to cross the border into Londonderry and attend school where lessons would be taught through the medium of English instead of Gaelic. So I began to make plans for our departure.

45 GOOD-BYE

PACKING up to leave Kenmare was the most heart-breaking thing I've ever experienced. All the neighbours helped and although I was against taking any furniture as it was worthless old stuff, everyone said that it would be impossible to buy more as the war had been on for so long, so they tied it up securely and took it to the station on their horse-cars. Then there were the animals to dispose of. I wanted to buy a caravan so that we could at least take the pony and Lassie, but the children were frightened at the idea; maybe they thought I was going to turn them into tinkers, or else they were afraid of the tinkers they would meet on the road.

So there was nothing else for it but to send for the Vet to have Lassie put down. She was too nervous a dog to take on the train; we took her only once to Kenmare and she was so scared of the traffic that she had another fit—the only one since the beginning—and scaled a twenty-foot wall and disappeared for three days. Everyone had a dog of their own and no one wanted Lassie. Besides she would only allow the family to go near her and would have bitten anyone else. I imagined her standing day after day and week after week waiting for our return—as she always did if we even went to Kenmare for the day.

As the Vet said her death would be painless, we decided it was kinder that way. To make her docile he first of all gave her a saucer of milk with a sedative in it but it only made her bleary-eyed; after another dose she walked around the kitchen trying not to fall over and determined not to let go. When he injected her shoulder she dropped on to the floor and squirmed about looking awful. At this point Stella and I had had enough—Joey was out playing at the Barry's, thank goodness, so we ran upstairs to wait until it was all over. We were looking out of the back window and to our horror we saw the Vet dragging Lassie by her hind legs, her head bumping over the rough ground, her mouth in a grimace and her tongue lolling out. He pulled her into the hen-house and shut the door behind him, leaving Stella and I bawling into the pillows. I don't know what happened in there; all I know is that when I went in later, the floor was covered in blood and a spade, also covered in blood, was leaning up against the wall.

I felt as though I had murdered her and for months after her terrible death haunted me.

Then there was the cat. No one would have her either. She was a wild thing, full of fear, so I thought I had better put her down myself by first of all giving her chloroform, then drowning her in the sea. It was altogether ghastly!

The cows were the next to go; Tara was bought and taken away the same evening to the amazement of the other cow, Rosaleen. They had never been parted for a minute for over three years and Rosaleen couldn't understand what was happening when she was left inside and Tara taken out on to the road. She ran up and down bellowing and trying to push her way through the hedge, and all through the night she bellowed. Thank goodness, she was sold the next day. After we had left, I was told that both cows had been seen several times on the road at the bottom of the land. I suppose they were looking for each other.

The donkeys were sold next, to different people, and they too were often seen on the land afterwards. Shamrock, the pony, was the only one we felt happy about. She was sold to one of the neighbours and was quite content to go along with him.

The hens were the next to dispose of and as they had reverted to their wild state long ago, it was impossible to catch them. The Dummy, the deaf and dumb boy from the shop where we dealt, was sent up; there wasn't a single job that he couldn't do but he wasn't able to catch the hens. He placed each one of us at various positions in the field and gave us instructions with the only two words he could say, "Ummer, ummer," and although we understood him perfectly, he only caught one small chicken and that was by standing on it in a bed of ferns and as he couldn't hear it cheeping I had to push him off it. It was so badly hurt I felt quite sick and when he picked it up I pulled him to the stream and indicated to drown it, he looked puzzled and then putting his head back he began imitating a chicken drinking, thinking that I meant "give it a drink." No, no," I said, pointing to the water. Again he looked puzzled and flung it over on the opposite bank and was walking away. In the end I had to drag him by the hand and make him hold it under the water until it drowned.

We went into the house and wrote on every available piece of paper. He had been taught by the Jesuits in Dublin and could write beautifully without any spelling mistakes, which was more than I was able to do. He wrote that he would catch the hens when it was dark and they had gone to roost up the trees, and for the next two hours his stories kept us amused. He said he had got to know many deaf and dumb girls up in Dublin but most of them were common; they spoke with two hands instead of the educated way with one only.

When darkness came he climbed up the hawthorn tree and grabbed one of the hens by the leg but that was the only one he caught; the rest took wing when they heard all the squawking, and settled up the high pine trees in Doyle's land.

Then I had an idea born out of desperation. I went to the chemists and bought enough bromide to put a man to sleep for three days. I mixed it in with their food and waited with a sack ready to go round picking up the somnolent hens, but they didn't turn a feather, only went on the same as always. Murty Sullivan said we were "mad out" and he would soon have them caught so he and his brother came down the next day with three of their dogs and spent the whole of the afternoon stalking hens, the dogs yelping so excitedly it sounded like a day out hunting with the "Galway Blazers" but they didn't catch one. When we left, hundreds of hens up in the branches of the trees watched us leave them for ever to their fate. Later, the Sullivan brothers came down with guns and shot them like they would wild birds, which of course they were.

At last the day came when we were to leave. Everyone from round about came to the station to see us off. I felt as though we were off to America like so many others before. We leant out of the train window, joking and laughing with everyone, then, through her laughter, I saw Mrs Sullivan wipe away a tear with the back of her hand. Mrs Doyle, with a wry smile, began dropping tears on to her coat. Bina-up-the-mountain started next, bawling loudly and saying "Don't go!" This set Stella off, and she was so overcome, she ran into the corridor and she never looked out again. The train started to move, leaving everyone standing on the platform, laughing and crying and waving good-bye. And Stella, the only one of us who wanted to leave Kenmare, was worse than anyone. She didn't dry her eyes until we reached Dublin City.

THE END